THE CATHOLIC UNIVERSITY OF AMERICA
CANON LAW STUDIES

No. 245

Ignorance Affecting Matrimonial Consent

A DISSERTATION

Submitted to the Faculty of the School of Canon Law of the Catholic University of America in Partial Fulfillment of the Requirements for the Degree of Doctor of Canon Law

BY THE
REV. VINCENT MICHAEL SMITH, S.T.L., J.C.L.
Priest of the Archdiocese of Philadelphia

THE CATHOLIC UNIVERSITY OF AMERICA PRESS, INC.
WASHINGTON, D. C.
1950

Nihil Obstat:

(Rev.) John Rogg Schmidt,
Censor Librorum deputatus ad hoc.

Washingtonii, D. C., die 19 augusti 1948.

Imprimatur:

✠ D. Card. Dougherty,
Archiepiscopus Philadelphiensis.

Philadelphiae, die 20 augusti 1948.

The Walther Printing House
Philadelphia, Pennsylvania

TABLE OF CONTENTS

PART II

CANONICAL COMMENTARY

FOREWORD

The present study endeavors to present a historical and canonical treatment of the question of ignorance as affecting matrimonial consent. It aims to indicate the requisite mental capacity for the eliciting of matrimonial consent, and to that end considers the mental state and the intellectual maturity of the contracting parties as well as their understanding of the individual essential elements which together constitute the marriage contract.

As is indicated in the table of contents the work is divided into two sections. The first section traces briefly the legal history of ignorance in its nature of a hindrance to matrimonial consent, with consideration given to both the theory of the canonists and the practice of the ecclesiastical courts, and note taken of the development and clarification wrought by the application to specific cases of the prohibition against ignorance as a hindrance to marriage. The second section is devoted to a canonical commentary on the effect of ignorance on matrimonial consent as mentioned in canon 1082.

To indicate more clearly the necessity for knowledge in order that a matrimonial consent may be given, ignorance is taken in its broadest sense, so that the concept includes ignorance as resulting from a state of the mind in which mental activity is impossible or at least impaired, and ignorance in accordance with the strict sense of the definition, connoting the lack of knowledge in a subject capable of and constituted for possessing knowledge.

The practical value of the question lies in the fact that ignorance as a hindrance to consent has its foundation in the natural law, so that ignorance can be said to vitiate any marriage contract whether the contracting parties are Catholics, non-Catholics, or infidels. If they are ignorant of the essential elements of the contract, they do not give a valid consent to marry.

The writer wishes to express his gratitude to His Eminence, Dennis Cardinal Dougherty, Archbishop of Philadelphia, for the opportunity of advanced study in Canon Law; to the Faculty of the School of Canon Law; and to all those who contributed by their interest and aid towards the completion of this dissertation.

TO MY FATHER

PART ONE

HISTORICAL SYNOPSIS

CHAPTER I

LEGISLATION BEFORE THE COUNCIL OF TRENT

The advent of the Christian era and the subsequent elevation of marriage to the dignity of a sacrament gave new impetus to matrimonial legislation.[1] Marriage by virtue of its sacramental character was brought under the exclusive jurisdiction of the Church.[2] It fell to the Church, therefore, to provide for its protection by means of adequate legislation. Thus in the course of time legal foundation was given to every notion pertaining to the marriage state. It was unlikely that consent, the efficient cause of the marriage contract, and the obstacles to the eliciting of a valid consent would be overlooked.

The subject of ignorance affecting matrimonial consent as the content of canon law cannot be attributed to any precise enactment or to any definite period of ecclesiastical legislation. The history of Church Law rather points to the application of a presupposed principle to particular cases, and traces the scientific development of that principle to a determination of the specific knowledge required for matrimonial consent.

1 Conc. Trident., sess. VII, *de sacramentis in genere,* can. 1; sess. XXIV, de matrimonio, proemium, can. 1 — Mansi, *Sacrorum Conciliorum Nova et Amplissima Collectio* (53 vols. in 60, Parisiis, Arnhem-Leipzig, 1901-1927), XXXIII, 52, 150. (Hereafter cited *Mansi.)*

2 Pius VI, const. *Auctorem fidei,* 28 aug. 1794, prop. 58, Synodi Pistoriensis, damn. — *Codicis Iuris Canonici Fontes cura Emi Petri Card. Gasparri editi* (9 vols., Romae postea Civitate Vaticana: Typis Polyglottis Vaticanis, 1923-1939; Vols. VII-IX, ed. cura et studio Emi Iustiniani Card. Seredi), n. 475 (hereafter cited *Fontes).*

Article I — Contingent Ignorance

A. *Persons of Defective Mentality*

According to Roman Law, an insane person of either sex was unable to contract marriage, but when marriage was already contracted it was not to be annulled in consequence of subsequent insanity.[3] The principle that an insane person is incapable of contracting marriage was adopted and canonized by ecclesiastical authority,[4] since it was evident that persons of unsound mind were incapable of giving a valid consent, without which there could be no marriage. The reason for the impossibility of a valid consent was given in an argument contained in the *Glossa*. The Glossator argued that an act of the will could not be placed by one who did not know what he was doing.[5] Therefore, without the operation of a sound mind and the knowledge which is its product no consent was possible.

The principle was confirmed by Innocent III, who applied it to a specific case. It was made known to the Pontiff that a certain man had unwittingly given his daughter in marriage to a youth who was insane. The woman was unable to live with the man because of his mental condition, and Innocent was asked to dissolve the union. He replied that because of the condition of insanity a legitimate consent was not given, and therefore the parties were to be separated.[6]

3 *Sententiae Pauli,* XIX, 7 — *Fontes Iuris Romani Antejustiniani* (Florentiae: apud G. Barbera, 1908), p. 283.

4 C. 26, C. XXXII, q. 7 — *Corpus Iuris Canonici* (ed. Lipsiensis 2., post Aemilii L. Richteri curas instruxit Aemilius Freidberg, 2 vols., Lipsiae: Ex Officina Bernhardi Tauchnitz, 1879-1881. Ed anastice repetita, Lipsiae: Tauchnitz, 1928); Jaffé, *Regesta Pontificum Romanorum ab condita ecclesia ad annum post Christum natum MCXCVIII* (2. ed. cura Wattenbach, Kaltenbrunner, Ewald, Loewenfeld, 2 vols., Lipsiae, 1885-1888), n. 80 (hereafter cited as *Jaffé).*

5 *Glossa Ordinaria,* ad c. 26, C. XXXII, q. 7, s. v. *contrahere;* c. 1, 2, C. XV. q. 1.

6 C. 24, X, *de sponsalibus et matrimoniis,* IV, 1; Potthast, *Regesta Pontificum Romanorum inde ab anno post Christum natum MCXCVIII ad annum MCCCIV* (2 vols., Berolini, 1874-1875), n. 2634 (hereafter cited as *Potthast).*

The words of the Pontiff declaring the marriage invalid clearly indicated that defective knowledge constituted the ultimate grounds for the separation. Innocent declared that consent could not be given because of the mental aberration *(propter alienationem furoris)*. The aberration stood in the way of the normal mental process, and the consequent ignorance forestalled all possibility of the human character of the act.

His reasoning was borne out by the *Glossa,* where a more extensive explanation of the case was given. Bernard of Parma (†1266) wrote that if during a lucid moment the insane party had given consent the marriage was valid, and the parties could not be separated. This was true, because during a period of sanity, no matter how brief, the party then in possession of his faculties could have sufficient knowledge to institute a valid consent, and therefore to contract a valid marriage. Otherwise the woman who contracted marriage with a man of unsound mind was not bound by the contract.[7] However, if the condition of insanity arose only subsequent to the marriage contract, the union could not be dissolved. If both parties were of sound mind at the time when the marriage was contracted, the consent given was valid, and the later mental defect could destroy neither the consent nor the bond. Rufinus (†1190) thus explained the prohibition against separation as contained in the alleged decree of Pope Fabian. Separation was prohibited when marriage had been contracted and consummated before the party became insane.[8] In any case the inference is clear that the determining factor is the consent of the parties made possible through knowledge.

The commentaries on the decretals of Gregory IX gave further elucidation to the relation between knowledge and matrimonial consent. In fact, it was with the writings of Hostiensis

7 "Si per delucida intervalla redit ad sanam mentem, et tunc contrahit, tenetur ad matrimonium." — *Glossa Ordinaria,* ad c. 24, X, *de sponsalibus et matrimoniis,* IV, I, s. v. *Furore.*

8 "(Non separantur si contraxisset) antequam insaniret, et copula perfectum." — Rufinus, *Summa Decretorum* (ed. H. Singer, Paderborn, 1902), c. 26, C. XXXII, q. 7.

(†1271) that theoretical arguments against the validity of consent affected by ignorance began to come into prominence. Hostiensis argued for the invalidity of consent from an analysis of consent itself. Gratian had defined consent as the agreement of two or more persons on the same thing.[9] Hostiensis used this analysis or definition to prove that a valid consent was foreign to one who was insane, for when the mind was without intellectual knowledge, and when absolute ignorance obscured the activity of the will, then there could be no such agreement.[10] Henricus Boich (1310-1350) extended the invalidating effect on matrimonial consent to every type of accidental ignorance. While commenting on the problem of marriage and insanity, he considered as a parallel case the possibility of contracting marriage on the part of one in the state of absolute drunkenness. If the state of inebriety was so complete that the use of reason was entirely taken away, then marriage was impossible, because consent could not be given. Thus one who was otherwise normally endowed with all the qualities and requisites for giving a valid matrimonial consent was deemed incapable of doing so when interference with the natural faculties resulted in ignorance.[11]

B. *Deaf-Mutes*

The application of the principle that ignorance stood in the way of matrimonial consent was further extended to include deaf-mutes. Pope Innocent III (1198-1216) had declared that mutes could contract marriage, since they could formulate a valid consent.[12] His argument in favor of his decision contained a comparison between mutes and children. This comparison

9 Consensus est sensus duorum vel plurium in idem." — *Dictum Gratiani*, C. XXIX, q. 1.

10 Hostiensis (Henricus de Segusio), *Commentaria in Quinque Decretalium Libros* (5 vols. in 3, Venetiis, 1581), c. 14, *de spons. et matr.*, IV, I, n. 5 (hereafter cited *Hostiensus).*

11 Boich, *Commentaria in Quinque Decretalium Libros* (Venetiis, 1576), c. 24, *de spons. et matr.*, IV, I, n. 4.

12 C. 23, X, *de sponsalibus et matrimoniis*, IV, 1.

implied, at least, that ignorance was a hindrance to consent and to marriage. Innocent declared that mutes, although they could not give verbal expression to their consent, could contract marriage, since a verbal expression was not a *conditio sine qua non* for consent. Children, on the other hand, although capable of pronouncing the words required by the marriage form, were readily understood not to give matrimonial consent.[13] For children, although gifted with speech, lack the necessary knowledge which mutes could have.[14]

The problem of physical defect in relation to knowledge and matrimonial consent was taken up by the commentators who investigated theoretically the physical condition of the parties to determine the possible existence of a hindrance to the marriage. Hostiensis proposed a case dealing with one who was born deaf, dumb, and blind. Such a person, he thought, seemed to have no way of knowing anything about marriage, and for that reason to be unable to consent to a marital union.[15] He went further to stress the importance of knowledge by holding out the hope of marriage through the possibility of giving consent in view of one's enlightenment by natural reason and the promptings arising from the sensations consequent to puberty. With such knowledge and consciousness he believed consent could be given.[16] The same case was treated by Panormitanus (1389-1453), who seemed to deny to deaf-mutes the possibility of a valid consent. For even if the deaf-mute could have a natural knowledge of woman through his natural reason, his natural

13 C. 25, X, *de sponsalibus et matrimoniis*, IV, 1.

14 "Consensum non habent [impuberes] quia aetas illa ignorat quid videat." — *Glossa Ordinaria*, ad c. 25, X, *de sponsalibus et matrimoniis*, IV, 1, s. v. *non contrahunt*.

15 Si caecus fuerit a nativitate, et mutuus et surdus, de tali non videtur quod possit contrahere, quia nunquam vidit matrimonium contrahi, nec uxorem teneri. Et sic in eo quod nunquam viderit, nec scit quid sit, consentire non potest." — Hostiensis, ad c. 23, *de spons. et matr.*, IV, I, n. 3.

16 "Etiam videtur, quia talis cognoscere potest mulierem, et naturali utitur ratione, si stimulus carnis incitatus, turpia signa . . . ostenderet, per quae evidenter apparet quod mulierem quaerebat . . ." — Hostiensis, *loc. cit.*

knowledge was not sufficient for the purpose of contracting matrimony.[17]

ARTICLE II — SUBSISTENT IGNORANCE

A. *Children*

According to law children were excluded from the marriage state.[18] To contract marriage validly three things were necessary: consent to form the contract, the development achieved through puberty, and the possession of the requisite potency to fulfill its obligations.[19] Children were deficient in all three respects. Puberty and potency were evidently wanting in children, since their lack of age precluded the presence of these natural endowments. Consent was also lacking, and a study of this deficiency of consent reveals that ignorance was its cause.

Gratian declared that for the validity of a contract, since it was effected by consent, it was necessary that both parties should know what they were doing.[20] For that reason parents who gave their children in marriage before they reached the age of puberty effected nothing, unless the children themselves upon reaching the age of discretion ratified the contract by their own consent.[21]

17 "De muto et surdo et caeco simul, nunquid possint matrimonium contrahere. Primo videtur quod sic, quia naturaliter potest mulierem cognoscere, etiam habet rationem naturalem. In contraria, quia nunquam vidit matrimonium contrahi nec audivit, et sic cum ignoret quid sit matrimonium, non videtur quod possit consentire in matrimonium." — Panormitanus, *Commentaria in Quinque Libros Decretalium* (5 vols. in 7, Venetiis, 1588), c. 23, *de spons. et matr.*, IV, I, n. 6.

18 C. 2, X, *de desponsatione impuberum*, IV, 2.

19 "Ad matrimonium autem contrahendum tria exiguntur, consensus, et quod sit pubes, et ad coeundum potens." — *Glossa Ordinaria*, ad *Dict. Grat.*, C. XXX, q. 2, s. v. *sponsalia*.

20 "Solo enim consensu contrahuntur, qui intervenire non potest, nisi ab alterutra parte id intelligatur, quod inter eos agitur." — *Dictum Gratiani*, c. un., C. XXX, q. 2.

21 "Ubi non est consensus utriusque non est conjugium. Ergo qui pueris dant puellas in cunabulis, et e converso, nihil faciunt nisi uterque puerorum, postquam venerit ad annos discretionis, consentiat." — C. un., C. XXX, q. 2.

Gratian did not raise the question of puberty or potency. The determining factor upon which he insisted was the consent or the lack of consent due to a sufficiency or a deficiency of knowledge. The *Glossa* interpreted the mind of Gratian accordingly by declaring that consent was impossible in children below the age of puberty, since the age indicated was not sufficient to permit one to suppose the existence of the necessary knowledge.[22]

Moreover, the dictum indicated the age of discretion as the time when consent could be given. That age, according to Rufinus, was fourteen years for boys and twelve for girls, the respective ages when both parties by reason of their physical development could have sufficient knowledge for the contracting of marriage.[23] Use of reason was not enough. There was needed the specific knowledge peculiar to the age of puberty. This was an important point, implied indeed in the previous legislation, but further clarified by Rufinus. By so designating the age of discretion he was preparing the way for the specification of sufficient knowledge, that knowledge which in a qualitative and quantitative analysis would suffice to effect a matrimonial consent.

Although marriage between children was impossible because of the lack of sufficient physical and intellectual development, it was customary for parents to arrange for the marriages of their children by means of promises which were held to be binding even on the children until they reached the age of puberty, at which time they could either give their consent and thereby marry, or break the promise.[24] Extensive legislation was enacted to cover these arrangements or espousals, as they were called,

22 "Aetas illa nesciat quid videat." — *Glossa Ordinaria*, ad *Dict. Grat.*, C. XXX, q. 2, s. v. *sponsalia.*

23 "Ipsae autem nuptiae non nisi inter puberes celebrari possunt, ut scilicet masculus sit XIV annorum, femina vero XII. . . . Si ante annos discretionis, i. e. quartum decimum vel duodecimum consenserit, non valet, nisi postea consensus ille confirmetur." — Rufinus, *Summa Decretorum*, c. un., C. XXX, q. 2.

24 Alexander III (1159-1181), Episcopo Bathonensi, c. 8, X, *de desponsatione impuberum*, IV, 2; Jaffé, n. 13765.

and in connection with this legislation further proof of the effect of ignorance on consent is to be found.

Alexander III (1159-1181) decreed that a promise to marry could not be broken by the parties to the contract before they reached the legitimate age for marriage.[25] His decree was based on the principle that one who could not consent likewise could not dissent. So also did Panormitanus argue, stating that, since children did not have a sufficient knowledge to give consent to a perpetual union, therefore they could not depart from a promised union until they understood what the union entailed.[26] The Abbot's statement represented the clearest expression of the prohibitive force of ignorance as found in this period. It showed that consent was lacking in children below the age of puberty precisely because of ignorance.

Legislation concerning the age of the contracting parties supplied another authoritative source which indicated, although indirectly, the nullifying effect of ignorance in matrimonial consent. When the law demanded the completion of the fourteenth and the twelfth years for boys and girls respectively,[27] it was because those ages were indicative of the age of discretion as far as marriage was concerned. The attainment of these respective ages laid the basis for a presumption not only in favor of puberty with the necessary physical endowments, but also in favor of the presence of the spiritual faculties postulated for the effecting of a matrimonial contract.[28]

The determining factor of legitimate age, therefore, was not primarily the completion of a certain number of years, but the physical and mental development of the contracting parties, so much so that, if one had not yet reached the numerical age prescribed by law, but was capable of coition and possessed of the necessary knowledge, he could contract marriage validly.[29]

25 C. 7, X, *de desponsatione impuberum,* IV, 2; Jaffé, n. 13767.

26 "Non videtur quod quis [impubes] habeat perfectum sensum ad consentiendum indissolubiliter in futurum matrimonii." — Panormitanus, *op. cit.*, c. 7.

27 C. 3, 6, X, *de desponsatione impuberum,* IV, 2.

28 C. 3, 6, X, *de desponsatione impuberum,* IV, 2.

29 "Duplex distinguitur pubertas, alia legalis (14 annor. aetas pro viris,

Alexander III declared that a marriage was not to be dissolved because of lack of age when it was evident that a valid consent could at the time be given in view of the precocity of the contracting party. In such a case the precocity *(malitia)* supplemented the minor age.[30] Precocity *(malitia)*, according to Panormitanus, signified natural power or potency, but it included also sufficient knowledge, for the Abbot qualifyingly declared that the capacity for effecting coition sufficed for the contracting of marriage as long as the parties understood the nature of matrimony.[31] Marriage was contracted through the consent of the parties; therefore knowledge was necessary.

B. *Adults*

Although early legislation was confined, for the most part, to cases involving children and abnormal adults, there was an indication that ignorance could vitiate the consent of normal adults as well. Knowledge was not the necessary complement of the acknowledged legitimate age. Even as the possession of this age did not necessarily evince the attainment of puberty, so also neither the achieved age nor the attained puberty necessarily vouched for the presence of sufficient knowledge. Panormitanus echoed this truth when he wrote that both knowledge and age were requisite factors for the validity of marriage.[32]

12 annor. pro mulieribus), alia physiologica (i. e. copulae capacitas cum mentis dicretione ad consensum matrimonialem necessaria); si haec adesset, illa adhuc deficiente, matrimonium validum erat." — Lanza, *Theologia Moralis Specialis de Matrimonio* (Romae, 1940), p. 457.

30 "Si ita fuerint aetati proximi, quod poturerint copula carnali coniungi, minoris aetatis intuitu ab invicem separari non debent, si unus in alium visus fuerit consensisse, quia in eis aetatem supplevisse malitia videtur." — C. 9, X, *de desponsatione impuberum,* IV, 2; Jaffé, n. 13969.

31 "Malitia intelligitur vigor naturae seu potentia coeundi. . . . Proximitas aetati non sufficit sine potentia coeundi, sed potentia coeundi bene sufficit sine proximitate, dummodo sint doli capaces, et quod potuerint discernere vires matrimonii, nam matrimonium non contrahitur ex copula, sed ex consensu." — Panormitanus, *op. cit.,* c. 9, *de despons. impub.*, IV, 2, n. 4.

32 "Duo quae requiruntur ad validitatem matrimonii, scientia, scilicet, et aetas." — Panormitanus, *op. cit.*, c. 7, *de spons. et matr.*, IV, I, n. 1.

Alexander III, in a decision given to the Archbishop of Canterbury, had shown that a party to a contract could be bound only in accordance with the ordinary understanding of the terms of the contract. Positing the necessity for knowledge and age, the Pope had indicated that if one party to an espousal did not fully understand the proposition of the other, he was bound only in accordance with the measure of his understanding.[33]

The same principle applied to the marriage contract. If the understanding was deficient regarding some essential element of the contract, then there was no true consent, and in consequence also no marriage.[34]

33 C. 7, X, *de sponsalibus et matrimoniis,* IV, 1; Jaffé, n. 13793.

34 The Glossator applied the principle to marriage as well as to espousals, declaring that an investigation should be made to see "si matrimonium contracturi ad id faciendum sint idonei scientia et aetate." — *Glossa Ordinaria,* ad c. 7, X, *de sponsalibus et matrimoniis,* IV, 1.

CHAPTER II

JURIDIC DOCTRINE FROM THE COUNCIL OF TRENT TO THE CODE OF CANON LAW

ARTICLE I — DEVELOPMENT OF LAW RELATIVE TO CONTINGENT IGNORANCE

For the greater part of this period the development of the legislation regarding the factor of ignorance was confined to a consideration of those subjects who were unable to give consent because of a physical or mental defect which precluded or impaired intellectual activity and due deliberation. This development was independent of any new positive legislation on the part of the Church. Innocent III had decreed that insane persons could not marry, since their mental state interfered with the necessary consent.[1] The same pontiff had declared that mutes were not to be denied the right to marry, as long as they could consent to a union.[2] These decrees together with the prohibition attributed to Pope Fabian I[3] were the basic norms for the subsequent decision in all cases of contingent ignorance. The decretalists and the doctors of the law, whose duty it was to pass judgment on cases introduced into the ecclesiastical courts, merely explained and interpreted these laws in accordance with their particular application.

A. *The Doctrine of the Decretalists*

According to the unanimous consent of the post-Tridentine decretalists two things were required for the marriage contract, namely, knowledge whereby the contracting parties might know

1 C. 24, X, *de sponsalibus et matrimoniis,* IV, 1 Potthast, n. 2634.

2 C. 25, X, *de sponsalibus et matrimoniis,* IV, 1, Potthast, n. 2656.

3 "Neque furiosus neque furiosa matrimonium contrahere possunt; sed si contractum fuerit, non separentur." — c. 26, C. XXXII, q. 7; Jaffé, n. 80. Jaffé indicates that this decree is spurious.

what they were doing, and freedom whereby they could place their act without hindrance.[4] Lack of deliberation, therefore, was opposed to the marriage contract and rendered it invalid. A defect in deliberation, according to Sanchez (1550-1610), could be attributed to the act itself — because it was placed hurriedly and without premeditation — in which case, although the contracting parties had a habitual knowledge of the essential elements of matrimony, the marriage would nevertheless be invalid, because the very act by which the contract was made was placed without deliberation; or it could be attributed to the subject, inasmuch as the subject was incapable of performing any human act.[5]

Furthermore, the inability to give matrimonial consent on the part of the subject could arise from a physical or a mental defect, or, as Sanchez stated, in view of the fact that the subject was devoid of the use of reason, or was deprived of the use of those senses whereby he might be taught the nature of the contract.[6]

Since he was incapable of deliberation, an insane person was unable to perform any human act. Therefore he could not validly contract marriage.[7] The note of invalidity arose in this case not because of any injury done to the party who unknowingly married one who was insane, but because the consent whereby the contract was to be effected could not be given by one so afflicted. Consequently, even if the one party knew of the abnormal mental state of the other, the contract was invalid.[8]

Anyone who wished to impugn the validity of a marriage on

4 Cf. *Acta Sanctae Sedis* (41 vols., Romae, 1865-1908), XXI (1885), 149.

5 "Defectus autem deliberationis potest ex duplici causa oriri: aut ex parte ipsius actus, quia subito et impremeditato motu gestus est; aut ex parte subjecti, quia deliberandi incapax est." — Sanchez, *De Sancto Matrimonii Sacramento* (3 vols. in 2, Antverpiae, 1607), lib. I, disp. VIII, n. 1.

6 Sanchez, *loc. cit.*

7 Covarrubias, *Opera Omnia* (2 vols., Coloniae Allobrogum, 1679), pars II, c. II, n. 6.

8 Covarrubias, *ibidem*, n. 8; Sanchez, *op. cit.*, lib. I, disp. VIII, n. 15.

the basis of insanity had to prove that the party was insane at the time when the marriage was contracted. There was a presumption among men in favor of the sanity of the parties, and consequently in support of the validity of their marriage. This was so because sanity was the natural state of all men; a contrary condition had to be proved.[9] Moreover, according to Sanchez, for a valid act of matrimonial consent, a party had to be proved capable of only that deliberation which would be sufficient for the commission of mortal sin. With that amount of deliberation availing for a party the contracting of marriage was possible; without it there could not be any contract.[10]

The decretalists made it clear that insanity was an obstacle to marriage only when it was concomitant with the issuance of the consent. If a party enjoyed lucid intervals, and gave his consent while of sound mind, the consent was true and the contract valid.[11]

A difficulty could arise, however, when there was a doubt whether the consent was given during a period of sanity or while the party was still devoid of reason. Covarrubias (1512-1577) set down a series of norms whereby this doubt might be resolved.

(1) If a person was known to have been insane over a period of time, such as a month or a year, it was presumed that he performed his acts while in the state of insanity. However, if the stigma of insanity extended only to a certain number of his acts, then it was not presumed that his unbalanced mental condition had continued, and in consequence the consent given by him was presumed to be valid.

(2) Insanity was presumed to influence those acts which were performed shortly after a period of insanity, not, however, those which were done a long time after recovery, or during a long interval of sanity.

9 "Natura ipsa homines sanae mentis producit." — Sanchez, *ibidem,* n. 17; Covarrubias, *ibidem,* n. 6.

10 Sanchez, *loc. cit.*

11 Covarrubias, *op. cit.,* pars II, c. II, n. 6; Sanchez, *op. cit.,* lib. I, disp. VIII, n. 17; Pirhing, *Ius Canonicum Nova Methodo Enplicatum* (5 vols. in 4, Dilingae, 1674-1678), lib. IV, tit. I, sect. I, n. 10.

(3) Insanity was not presumed to endure when in the opinion of physicians or psychiatrists the insanity had its roots in an accidental cause which had since been removed.

(4) If a person enjoyed lucid moments in which he was certainly of sound mind, and thereupon a doubt arose whether his act was performed while he was of sound mind or in a mentally defective state, the presumption for or against the validity of the act was to be based on the quality of the act itself and the circumstances surrounding it.[12]

These norms were accepted by the subsequent authors with one exception. When an act was of doubtful validity because of intermittent insanity, then the primary consideration, according to the later writers, was not to be given to the quality and circumstances of the act. Rather, there was to be an initial presumption against validity. Insanity was considered to be a continuous perpetual state; lucid intervals, on the other hand, were merely incidental. Consequently, all acts were to be presumed invalid until a consideration of the quality of the act and the circumstances surrounding it could build up a presumption for validity.[13]

The question then arose whether marriage could be contracted by virtue of an act of the will preceding the state of insanity. There was no doubt that a person could receive baptism, if, before he became insane, he had reflected the desire to receive the sacrament.[14] Could an insane person who, before he became insane, had the necessary knowledge and the will to marry, effect a valid contract? Sanchez denied the possibility.[15]

He argued that a minister who conferred the sacraments had to have an actual intention, and therefore had to be endowed with all the faculties required for the placing of a human act.

12 Covarrubias, *ibidem*, n. 7.

13 Sanchez, *op. cit.*, lib. I, disp. VIII, n. 17; Barbosa, *Collectanea Doctorum tam Veterum quam Recentorum in Ius Pontificium Universum* (5 vols., Lugduni, 1637), c. 34, *de sponsalibus et matrimoniis*, IV, I; Pirhing, *loc. cit.*

14 C. 3, X, *de baptismo et eius effectu*, III, 42; Potthast, n. 1479.

15 Sanchez, *ibidem*, n. 12.

Since the contracting parties were themselves the ministers of the sacrament of matrimony, their marriage was invalid if they contracted it while of unsound mind, even though a virtual intention resulting from a previous intention still endured.

Having given the rule, namely, that insanity impeded matrimonial consent, and having illustrated the application of the rule, the decretalists then began to look for and consider the exception to that rule. Sanchez found and admitted one exception, marriage by proxy. If a person became insane after he had given a mandate to a proxy to contract marriage, and his insanity endured even through the time when the proxy contracted the marriage in his name, then the marriage was valid.[16] The erstwhile consent given to the proxy continued to exist since it had never been revoked, and thereafter remained in force through the proxy. It was true that a person contracting through his own act had to be of sound mind; but it sufficed, when he contracted through a proxy, that he be of sound mind when he have his mandate, as long as the proxy was of sound mind when he furnished the consent of his principal. Even though the parties themselves, and not the proxy, were still the ministers of the sacrament, the contracted marriage was nevertheless valid, since the contracting party did not administer the sacrament by his own action, but did so instrumentally through the procurator.

Leurenius (1646-1723) reviewed the case as proposed and argued by Sanchez, but he did not reflect any positive inclination either to agree or to dissent from his doctrine.[17]

Pontius (1569-1629), however, did oppose the view of Sanchez. He denied that even in such circumstances the contracting of a valid marriage was at all possible.[18] The ultimate solution of this problem will be reserved to a later chapter.

Thus far only the insane, as mentioned in the decision of Innocent III and in the opinions of the post-Tridentine commen-

16 Sanchez, *ibidem*, n. 12.

17 Leurenius, *Ius Canonicum Universum* (3 vols., Venetiis, 1729), lib. IV, tit. I, q. 100.

18 Pontius, *De Sacramento Matrimonii Tractatus cum appendice de matrimonio Catholici cum heretico* (Bruxellis, 1627), lib. II, c. 15, n. 14.

tators, have been considered. The decretalists attached the same note of invalidity to marriages in which any mental defect stood in the way of the acquisition or possession of the knowledge necessary to constitute a valid consent. Consequently, whatever has been said of the insane party to a contract may be applied to any subject who is mentally deficient.[19] Any subject who was deprived of the use of reason, whether habitually or temporarily, could not validly marry as long as he continued in his abnormal state. Thus even those who entered into a contract while under the influence of alcoholic drink, or while in the heat of passion, were not bound by the union.[20]

As to the determination of a sufficient mental capability in such cases, the consensus of the authors indicated that only those who were capable of that deliberation which was sufficient for the commission of mortal sin could furnish a valid consent for marriage.[21] In other words, if a subject under the influence of intoxicants had nevertheless the mental capacity to commit mortal sin, he was considered mentally capable also of contracting marriage, inasmuch as it was supposed that he had a habitual knowledge regarding the subject-matter of the contract.

Aside from the mental defects which stood in the way of consent, there were physical defects which also could vitiate the consent of the parties. Such defects were those evidenced in the deaf, the dumb, and the blind.[22]

Innocent III had declared that, since consent simply of itself

19 Covarrubias, *op. cit.*, pars II, c. II, n. 1; Sanchez, *op. cit.*, lib. I, disp. VIII, n. 1; Pirhing, *op. cit.*, lib. IV, tit. I, sect. 1, n. 10.

20 Barbosa, *loc. cit.;* Leurenius, *op. cit.*, lib. IV, tit. I, q. 47.

21 "Constat a furioso nihil fieri posse, consensum liberum exigens qualem petunt sponsalia et matrimonium. Et idem dicendum est de mente capto, qui omnino usu rationis destituitur; secus est, si non caret omnino intellectu, quem vulgo 'tonto' appellamus: hic enim sponsalia et matrimonium inire potest: Ratio est manifesta, quia deliberationem sufficientem habet ad lethaliter delinquendum." — Sanchez, *op. cit.*, lib. I, disp. VII, n. 15; Reiffenstuel, *Ius Canonicum Universum* (7 vols., Parisiis, 1864-1870), lib. IV, tit. I, n. II.

22 Sanchez, *op. cit.*, lib. I, disp. VIII, n. 1, 13; Wex, *Doctrina Theoretico-practica SS. Canonum* (Dilingae, 1708), pars V, tract. II, c. III, n. 5.

sufficed for the contracting of a valid marriage, deaf-mutes should not be excluded from the marriage state.[23] They were to be deemed capable of giving a valid consent, since they were believed to be able through the use of signs to acquire the necessary knowledge for the contracting of a valid marriage.[24] However, if they were unable to learn in this way, but were dependent upon instinct alone for their knowledge of the marital union, they were equivalent to brute animals, and thus no appeal could be made to the decree of Innocent with a view to paving the way in support of the marriage as a valid union.[25]

With these facts in mind the decretalists investigated the various cases in which marriage could be declared valid or invalid in consideration of such physical defects.

In the first place no single physical defect could affect the validity of the consent. It was rather a combination of defects which could occasion the lack of knowledge.[26] Then, too, the acquisition of the necessary knowledge, and therefore the contracting of the marriage itself, was in no case of physical defect considered impossible. It was rather a question of greater or lesser probability, depending upon the mental resources of the individual.[27] Hence deaf-mutes were usually understood to have sufficient knowledge.[28] Those, on the other hand, who were deaf, dumb, and blind from birth were presumed to be incapable of acquiring a sufficient knowledge.[29] Sanchez likewise considered those who were deaf and blind from birth as incapable of acquiring a sufficient knowledge, since they were deprived of the ordinary means by which deaf-mutes could be taught the nature of marriage, namely, through the use of signs.[30]

23 C. 23, X, *de sponsalibus et matrimoniis,* IV, 1; Potthast, n. 329.

24 Sanchez, *loc. cit.*

25 Sanchez, *loc. cit.*

26 Sanchez, *loc. cit.;* Pirhing, *op. cit.,* lib. IV, tit. I, sect. I, n. II.

27 Sanchez, *ibidem,* nn. 12, 13, 14.

28 C. 23, X, *de sponsalibus et matrimoniis,* IV, 1; Sanchez, *ibidem,* n. 12.

29 Sanchez, *ibidem,* n. 13; Pirhing, *loc. cit.;* Wex, *loc. cit.*

30 Sanchez, *ibidem,* n. 14.

B. *Judicial Practice*

The nullifying effect of contingent ignorance was equally evident from the practice of the ecclesiastical courts. The Roman Rota and the Sacred Congregation of the Council, which had been called into being for the execution and the interpretation of the decrees of the Council of Trent, competent courts of the Roman Curia in matrimonial cases,[31] handed down declarations of nullity in marriage cases in which one of the contracting parties was devoid of rational knowledge.

Apropos of a decision given in 1624, the Rota declared that all persons who were deprived of the use of reason or of their senses were unable to enter into a marriage contract.[32] The same principle was expressed by the Sacred Congregation of the Council, which indicated that every mental malady which took away the use of reason was to be regarded as equivalent to insanity when the validity of a marriage contract was in question.[33] Therefore, it mattered not whether irrationality was predicable of a person's every act, or confined to those things only which pertained to marriage.[34] The deciding factor in every case was rather the presence or absence of the necessary knowledge for the giving of consent, due to the rational or irrational state of the mind.[35]

31 Hilling, *Procedure at the Roman Curia* (New York, 1907), pp. 64, 133.

32 "Furiosus, mente captus, ac sensu carens non possunt contrahere matrimonium, si ratione vel sensu omnino destitutus, perpetuo furore, vel defectu sensus laborat." — *Sanctae Romanae Rotae Decisiones coram Buratti* (Romae, 1624), annot. ad decis. 763.

33 S. C. C., *Treverin.*, 22, iul. 1899: "Etsi proprie et stricte demens, mente captus, differat a furioso, tamen latius pro synonimis habentur, ut cum furore dementia confundatur, et praesertim cum de valore matrimonii agatur." — *Thesaurus Resolutionum Sacrae Congregationis Concilii*, CLVIII (Romae, 1899), 680 (hereafter cited as *Thesaurus*).

34 S. R. R., *Nullitatis Matrimonii*, 9 apr. 1910, coram R. P. D. Gulielmo Sebastianelli, dec. XV, n. 2: "Neque refert si insania ad omnes vitae moralis actus extendatur (quo in casu vocatur amentia), vel ad unam vel alteram rem restringatur (quo in casu vocatur dementia): dementes enim, in iis circa quae insanirent, amentibus aequiparantur." — *S. R. R. Decisiones seu Sententiae*, II (1910), 145 (hereafter cited *S. R. R. Decisiones*).

35 S. R. R., *Nullitatis Matrimonii*, 15 maii 1915, coram R. P. D. Ioanne

The decisions of the courts indicated that there were different grades of mental states which could affect the consent of the parties. As a result consideration had to be given to each case to determine the extent of the abnormality and of the consequent ignorance. If a person was totally devoid of the use of reason, he was certainly excluded from the marriage state.[36] If, on the other hand, a person suffered from a mental defect without having lost completely the use of reason, he could give consent and contract marriage, as long as he was capable of that deliberation which was required for the commission of a mortal sin.[37]

These principles were followed regardless of the factors that caused or occasioned the mental states. If a person suffered the loss of the faculty of perception as a result of hereditary factors, as the effect of a nervous breakdown, or in consequence of a blow on the head, the issue was the same, the court declaring the marriage invalid because of defective consent.[38] In a decision granted in 1914, the Rota confirmed a declaration of nullity since it was proved that the man in the case had contracted marriage while delirious with fever.[39] Any cause, whether it produced a temporary or a habitual state of irrationality, could preclude a valid consent while its effect was present.

Before a mental condition could interfere with the marriage

Prior, dec. XX, n. 2: "Mutuo partium consensu matrimonium contrahitur, ad quem requiritur libera voluntatis electio, praeeunte cognitione rationali, uti in omni actu humano. Cum amentes incapaces sint eiusmodi cognitionis rationalis, consensum liberum praestare nequent, ac proinde a matrimonio contrahendo arcentur." — *S. R. R. Decisiones*, VII (1915), 217.

36 *S. R. R. Decisiones, loc. cit.*

37 S. R. R., *Nullitatis Matrimonii*, 15 maii 1915, coram R. P. D. Ioanne Prior, dec. XX, n. 4: "Qui semi-fatui sunt, seu semi-amentes, matrimonium valide contrahere possunt, dummodo deliberationi uti possunt, quae sufficit ad lethaliter peccandum." — *S. R. R. Decisiones*, VII (1915), 217.

38 S. R. R., *Nullitatis Matrimonii*, 1 apr. 1910, coram R. P. D. Gulielmo Sebastianelli, dec. XV, n. 2: "Quod enim insania sit ex hereditate, vel ex systematis nervosi generatione, vel ex vulnere forte in cerebro accepto, nihil prorsus refert, si tollat mentis preceptionem." — *S. R. R. Decisiones*, II (1910), 145.

39 S. R. R., *Nullitatis Matrimonii*, 23 mart. 1914, coram R. P. D. Gulielmo Sebastianelli, dec. XII — *S. R. R. Decisiones*, VI (1914), 144 sq.

contract, it had to be present at the time when the contract was made. Therefore, only those who were perpetually without the use of reason were forever excluded from the marriage state. When the mental condition was not continuous and perpetual, but admitted of intermittent periods of sanity, then a valid consent could be given during the period of rationality, for the impediment to consent was removed with the recovery of the rational faculty.

According to the general practice of the ecclesiastical tribunals, whenever an insane person enjoyed lucid intervals there existed no prohibition or disqualification to the contracting of a valid marriage; accordingly the marriage was valid.[40] But, if a doubt arose whether the contract was made during a lucid interval or during a period of insanity, the Rota recognized a presumption which favored the existence of insanity.[41]

This same presumption had been applied to a case reviewed by the Sacred Congregation of the Council. A certain Joseph de Guzman appealed to the Sacred Congregation for a declaration of nullity, since according to the testimony of witnesses his supposed wife was demented both before and after the celebration of the marriage.[42] The Congregation admitted the presumption which favored the existence of insanity as a basis for the appeal, but declared the marriage valid because of contrary proofs. The Sacred Congregation found from the proved facts of the case that the woman was of sound mind when the contract was made, and therefore able to give her consent.

Hence doubtful contracts of marriage were presumed to be invalid in the cases wherein insanity was, so to speak, in posses-

40 S. R. R., *Nullitatis Matrimonii*, 15 maii 1915, coram R. P. D. Ioanne Prior, dec. XX, n. 6: "Si amens lucida habet intervalla, et in his contrahit, matrimonium validum est." — *S. R. R. Decisiones*, VII (1915), 218.

41 "Probata enim amentia, pro ea praesumption militat, donec contrarium probetur." — *S. R. R. Coram Mantica, in Romana Donationis annuli*, 10 maii 1589.

42 S. C. C., *Corduben.*, 22 febr. 1763: "Cum testes deponat de Annae insania ante et post matrimonium, . . . insaniam contendit praesumendam esse pariter de tempore celebrati matrimonii."—*Thesaurus*, XXXII (1763), 39.

sion, and lucid intervals were incidental and infrequent occurrences. However, if the lucid intervals were very frequent, so that the periods of insanity rather than the sane intervals were considered to be incidental, the courts demanded very conclusive proofs of insanity as existing at the moment consent was given, for then there were no grounds for the initial presumption for insanity. The Sacred Congregation of the Council declared a marriage valid in just such a case, because of insufficient proof of the presence of a mental defect at the time of the marriage.[43]

As to physical defects which vitiate consent, the Rota declared that a person who was perpetually deprived of the use of his senses could not marry.[44] A clarification of this doctrine is found in a decision of the Rota given in 1764. The Rota placed the reason for the inability of such a person to contract marriage in the ignorance which resulted from the inactivity of the senses. The cited case deals with a deaf-mute who was capable of sense perceptions of the visible and material things which she saw and touched, but lacked the power of mentally apprehending things in their abstract nature. The Rota declared that marriage could not be contracted if such ignorance existed.[45]

Thus the judicial practice of the Sacred Congregation of the Council and of the Roman Rota confirmed the admitted incapacity for the contracting of marriage when the genuine giving of consent was voided by reason of a mental or a physical defect. By means of their decisions the courts made it clear that any defect which deprived a contracting party of the necessary and sufficient knowledge — the judicial sources do not reveal a more precise description of the knowledge required for the contracting

43 S. C. C. *Praemislien*, 24 mart. 1778: "Certum esse videtur ex dispositione testium examinatorum, hanc persaepe habuisse lucida mentis intervalla. Qua currente probatione, non licet eidem nullum dicere matrimonium, nisi concludentissime probet, ipsam tempore praeciso celebrati, matrimonii a recto mentis sensu fuisse prorsus alienam." — *Thesaurus*, XLVII (1778), 173.

44 *S. R. R. Decisiones coram Buratti*, anno 1624, decis. 763, ad annot.

45 "Si nullam habuisset ideam rerum abstractarum vel intellectualem, non potuisset certe matrimonium contrahere."—*S. R. R. Decisiones* (Romae, 1764), dec. XX, n. 12.

of marriage validly — thereby rendered his consent invalid. Accordingly, ignorance, no matter what may have been its incidental cause or occasion, stood in the way of a true consent, and therefore also of a valid marriage.

Article II — Development of Law Relative to Subsistent Ignorance

A. *Ignorance Regarding the Nature of the Matrimonial Contract in General*

Although the legislation which was directed against the prospective contracting of marriage by persons who were devoid of knowledge because of a physical or a mental defect sufficed to indicate the nullifying influence of ignorance in matrimonial consent, it was with the consideration of ignorance in the strict sense of the term, or ignorance as found in a normal subject who was capable of and constituted for the possession of knowledge, that the principle found its clearest expression.

Early in the post-Tridentine period, Sanchez (†1610) specifically singled out ignorance as an impediment to matrimonial consent. Taking his cue from the philosopher Aristotle, who wrote that nothing could be considered as flowing from an act of the will unless it was first presented to the will by the intellect, Sanchez declared that a marriage contract could not be effected in the presence of ignorance. Ignorance stood in the way of consent, and since the consent of the contracting parties was the efficient cause of the contract, ignorance likewise barred the formation and the existence of the contract itself.[46]

The same author and subsequent decretalists indirectly indicated the prohibitive force of ignorance in their treatment of the question of the legitimate age for the formation of a valid

46 "Ignorantia instar erroris impedit consensum efficitque ne actus sit voluntarius: nihil enim volitum quin praecognitum, teste Philosopho. Ignorantia cognitionem tollit, sicut error veram; unde quoad dirimendum matrimonium non differt an dicatur ignorantiam an errorem impedire." — Sanchez, *De Sancto Matrimonii Sacramento*, lib. VII, disp. XVIII, n. I.

matrimonial contract. The requisite age for marriage was fourteen and twelve years for boys and girls respectively. These ages were specified because they were considered to be indicative of the age of puberty.[47] But puberty, according to Gonzalez-Tellez († ca. 1673), was required for a valid marriage, inasmuch as only upon reaching the age of puberty were children considered as having the knowledge necessary for the giving of matrimonial consent, and possessing the power requisite for the begetting of offspring.[48] The ultimate determining factors inherent in the requirement of a legitimate age, therefore, were potency and knowledge, so much so that a person who was capable of begetting offspring, and possessed the necessary knowledge regarding the essence of the matrimonial contract, was qualified for the valid contracting of marriage even apart from having reached the specified age.[49]

This juridical fact was stressed quite clearly by Sanchez. Speaking of the necessity of complying with the law regarding the requisite age, he declared that a marriage contracted before the completion of the respective fourteenth and twelfth years

[47] "Deinde requiritur aetas legitima, nempe pubertatis, quae in masculo incipit post 14 annum, et foemina post 12, nisi malitia sive sagacitas naturae suppleat aetatem." — Pirhing, *Ius Canonicum,* lib. IV, tit. I, sect. I, n. 85.

[48] "Ratio autem propter quam pubertas ab utroque a jure in contrahendis nuptiis exigatur ex eo provenit, quia cum ad matrimonium contrahendum duo desiderentur, et discretio ad consensum explicandum, et facultas generandi: ideo quousque pubertas non adveniat, creditur impuberes ex defectu aetatis inutiles esse ad utrumque, videlicet consensum praestandum, et ad generandum, ac per consequens ad matrimonium contrahendum, cum deficiant consensus et facultas generandi, quae respiciunt substantiam et effectum matrimonii." — Gonzalez-Tellez, *Commentaria Perpetua in Singulos Textus Quinque Librorum Decretalium Gregorii IX* (5 vols. in 4, Lugduni, 1715), lib. IV, tit. II, c. 2, n. 7 (hereafter cited *Commentaria).*

[49] "Ad matrimonium contrahendum sola potentia coeundi sufficit, dummodo adsit vigor rationis ad discernedum vires matrimonii, quia pubertatem non metimur ex annorum numero." — Fagnanus, *Commentaria in Quinque Libros Decretalium* (4 vols., Romae, 1661), lib. IV, tit. II, c. 9, n. 8.

was valid, if the parties to the contract were both potent and endowed with sufficient knowledge.[50] The defect engendered in the lack of age could be overcome by precocity *(malitia)* on the part of the contracting parties,[51] as long as the concept of this precocity was extended to include both the factor of potency and also that of the correct understanding of the conjugal state and of the perpetual and indissoluble nature of the marital bond.[52]

The whole of the past legislation concerning the requisite age for the contracting of marriage shows that ignorance was considered as an impediment to the giving of consent, and therefore also the making of the marriage contract itself. Without potency and discretion no one was old enough to marry, whereas with potency and discretion one was able to marry whatever his age in years might be.

Judicial practice confirmed the teaching of the doctors both by admitting into court cases in which the discretion of the contracting parties was questioned, and by declaring invalid the marriages which had been contracted in ignorance.[53]

B. *Presumption of Law regarding Ignorance*

The determination of the legitimate age for the forming of a marriage contract gave rise to the presumption of law that a person who had reached the prescribed age had also a sufficient

50 "Validum est matrimonium ante aetatem jure praescriptum initum, si tunc adsit potentia generandi et sufficiens discretio ad se obligandum." —Sanchez, *op. cit.*, lib. VII, disp. CIV, n. 5.

51 "Potest evenire quod discretio habeatur ante dictam aetatem, quod jam fuit a jure provisum dicens, nisi malitia supplet aetatem."—Gonzalez-Tellez, *ibidem*, n. 5.

52 "Nomine malitiae communiter intelligunt doctores non tantum aptitudinem ad copulam conjugalem, seu potentiam generandi, sed etiam prudentiam, et judicium rationis sufficiens ad cognoscendum statum conjugalem, ejusque perpetuum et indissolubile vinculum." — Pirhing, *op. cit.*, lib. IV, tit. II, no. 37, ad 2.

53 S. C. C., *Csanadien.*, 18 dec. 1869 — *Thesaurus*, CXXVIII (1869), 649; *Ventimilien.*, 19 maii, 18 aug. 1888 — *Thesaurus*, CXLVII (1888), 289, 518; S. R. R., *Nullitatis Matrimonii*, 17 mart. 1910 coram R. P. D. Iosepho Mori, dec. XII. — *S. R. R. Decisiones*, II (1910), 112.

knowledge for the contracting of marriage.[54] Thus, one who had reached the age of puberty, that is, had completed the fourteenth or twelfth year, boys and girls considered respectively, was presumed to be in possession of the necessary knowledge for the contracting of a valid marriage.[55]

Sanchez' doctrine was even more liberal. He admitted a presumption in favor of knowledge when a person was very close to the age of puberty.[56] He took care, however, to distingunish between the physical ability for intercourse and the proximity to the age of puberty. Ability for the performance of the act of intercourse gave rise to a presumption in favor of potency, but not of discretion. On the other hand, proximity to the age of puberty furnished a juridical foundation for presuming the presence of the requisite knowledge, even though a person rarely was endowed with potency at such a time.[57]

The presumption of law in favor of knowledge had to yield to contrary proof. If a person was proved ignorant of the elements of marriage, even though he had passed the age determined by law as the time when by reason of both potency and

54 "Jus eam aetatem praescribit, quia praesumit tunc pueros, et non antea, esse praeditos et sufficienti judicio ad matrimonium contrahendum, et potentia generandi." — Sanchez, *op. cit.*, lib. VII, disp. CIV, no. 5; Pirhing, *op. cit.*, lib. IV, tit. II, n. 37, ad 4.

55 The cases reviewed by the Sacred Congregation and by the Roman Rota indicated the existence of such a presumption in law, particularly through the demands made by the courts for proof of ignorance. — Cf. *Thesaurus*, CXXVIII (1869), 656; CXLVII (1888), 304; *S. R. R. Decisiones*, II (1910), 115.

56 "Propinquitas pubertati facit praesumere discretionem sufficienter ad gravissimum ac perpetuum matrimonii vinculum contrahendum."—Sanchez, *op. cit.*, lib. VII, disp. CIV, n. 27.

57 "Copula nedum nisus ad illam copulam minime inducit praesumptionem discretionis ad matrimonium petitae; facit tamen praesumi potentiam. E' contra autem propinquitas pubertati facit praesumi discretionem, non tamen potentiam. In tenera aetate invenitur aliquando robur ad copulam, cum tamen in ea non solet tanta discretio adesse, quanta ad vinculum gravissimum ac perpetuum matrimonii desideretur. Et e contra, quando puer pubertati proxima est, solet discretione sufficienti ad hoc praeditus esse, cum tamen raro potentiam generandi tunc habeat."—Sanchez, *loc. cit.*

sufficient discretion one could marry, the presumption had to give way to truth.[58] The Sacred Congregation of the Council sustained this opinion by granting a declaration of nullity, when it proved that a girl, though she had passed the legitimate age, entered into a union without sufficient knowledge of the essential nature of the matrimonial contract. The Sacred Congregation declared that the marriage was invalid because of defective consent.[59]

C. *Extent of Invalidating Ignorance*

Thus far consideration has been given to the effect of ignorance in general on matrimonial consent. From such a discussion it must not be supposed that ignorance concerning any factor or element whatsoever pertinent to marriage or to the marriage contract sufficed to vitiate matrimonial consent, for with the marriage contract, as with any contract, only ignorance regarding the substantial elements of the contract could affect the validity of the marriage.[60]

Barbosa (†1649) had indicated as necessary that knowledge which reflected an understanding of the juridical force and implication of conjugal consent.[61] Pirhing (†1679), a little more

58 "Licet aetas duodecim et quatuordecim annorum communi et assiduo usu admissa sit; tamen si in illa aetate inhabiles reperiantur ad contrahendum, non sustinetur matrimonium inter eos celebratum; quia ea in re semper veritas attenta fuit, non juris praesumptio aut praescriptio." — Gonzalez-Tellez, *op. cit.*, lib. IV, tit. II, c. 2, n. 5.

59 S. C. C., *Ventimillien.*, 18 aug. 1888. — *Thesaurus*, CXLVII (1888), 518.

60 Pallottini, *Collectio omnium conclusionum et resolutionum quae in causis propositis apud Sacram Congregationem Cardinalium S. Concilii Tridentini interpretum prodierunt ab eius institutione anno MDLXIV ad annum MDCCCLX, distinctis titulis alphabetico ordine per materias digesta* (18 vols., Romae, 1868-1895), s. v. *Matrimonium*, III, *Quoad consensum*, n. 6 (hereafter cited as *Pallattini*).

61 "Requiritur copulative potentia ad carnalem copulam, necnon prudentia rationis ad sufficienter discernendum vim conjugalis consensus, nec satis est alterum tantum adesse." — Barbosa, *op. cit.*, lib. IV, tit. II, c. IX, n. 5.

explicit, required knowledge of the essence and nature of the conjugal state and its indissolubility.[62] However, it was not until the middle of the nineteenth century that the extent of the ignorance which sufficed to invalidate marriage was explicitly determined.

In 1856 there was brought on appeal from the archdiocese of Bamberg to the Sacred Congregation of the Council a case in which the validity of a marriage was impugned because of the ignorance of one of the contracting parties. A woman protested that she had no idea of the nature of carnal union, that is, of the physical use of marriage. The Sacred Congregation declared that such ignorance had no bearing on the validity of the contract. Carnal copulation did not pertain to the essence of the marriage, and ignorance thereof could not be said to vitiate the matrimonial consent.[63] Only ignorance of the substance of the contract precluded a valid consent, and accordingly a valid contract of marriage.[64] Therefore, according to the Sacred Congregation, it sufficed for the validity of the marriage if the contracting parties knew that marriage consisted in a mutual concession of the corporal rights of the married, and in a non-repudiation of its indissoluble bond.[65]

A similar decision was handed down by the same Sacred Congregation in 1869. A woman of the diocese of Csanád in Hungary sought a declaration of nullity, declaring that she

62 Pirhing, speaking of the precocity *(malitia)* which could substitute for the lack of age in a valid marriage contract, declared that precocity included the "potentia generandi, et prudentia, et judicium rationis sufficiens ad cognoscendum statum conjugalem, ejusque perpetuum, et indissolubile vinculum." — *op. cit.*, lib. IV, tit. II, n. 37, ad 2.

63 "Quod autem ipsa ignoret usum illius iuris consistere in coniunctione corporum per copulam carnalem, hoc non refert, quia non est de essentia matrimonii." — Pallottini, *loc. cit.*

64 "Ignorantia enim quae afficit validitatem matrimonii sicut et aliorum quorumcumque contractuum, ut norunt omnes, est illa, quae versatur circa substaniam, non vero circa qualitates, aliaque id genus." — Pallottini, *loc. cit.*

65 "Ad matrimonium sufficit, ut salventur fines essentiales seu matrimonii essentia, quae consistit in mutua traditione corporum quoad debitum, et in vinculo indissolubili." — Pallottini, *loc. cit.*

knew nothing of the conjugal obligations. She had accordingly refused to have intercourse with her husband, stating that such carnal intimacy was unworthy of human nature.[66]

The Sacred Congregation declared that ignorance of the essential obligations of marriage certainly nullified the marriage contract.[67] However, whatever was said of the effect of ignorance with regard to the essence of marriage, which namely consisted in the mutual concession of rights which entitled each to engage the body of the other for marital use, could in no way be applied to ignorance concerning carnal intercourse,[68] for matrimonial consent was not explicitly directed to a carnal union, but tended rather to the acknowledged possession of the right which made it lawful to request such a union; carnal copulation did not pertain to the essence of marriage, but was rather its effect.[69] Therefore, even a generic consent by which a person gave to and shared with another a rightful power over his own body, even apart from any specific reference to a carnal union, was sufficient to constitute a valid marriage.[70] Thus the Sacred Congregation made it clear that ignorance of the nature of carnal intercourse did not constitute an impediment to matrimonial consent. Ignorance was an impediment only when it was referable to the

66 S. C. C., *in Csanadien.*, 18 dec. 1869 — *Thesaurus*, CXXVIII (1869), 672.

67 "Facile est intelligere, non valere matrimonium quod contrahitur ab illa quae in huius essentiais obligationis sive ignorantia sive errore versatur." — *Thesaurus, loc. cit.*

68 "Attamen quod de ignorantia circa mutuam traditionem et potestatem corporum diximus nulla ratione dici potest de consensu in carnalem copu lam." — *Thesaurus, loc. cit.*

69 "Dicendum est consensum matrimonium constituentem non esse explicite in carnalem copulam sed in ius et potestatem ad talem copulam, quia carnalis copula non est de matrimonii essentia, sed eius effectus et operatio." — Sanchez, *De Sancto Matrimonii Sacramento*, lib. II, disp. XXVII, n. 3. — Quoted by the Sacred Congregation.

70 S.C.C., *in Csanadien.*, 18 dec. 1869: "Genericus consensus in mutuam corporum potestatem sufficit, neque ille speciatim, qui in carnalem copulam est, ad matrimonii valorem requiritur." — *Thesaurus*, CXXVIII (1869), 672.

marital rights and obligations — the very essence of marriage.[71]

Further elucidation was given by Gasparri (1852-1934). He declared that marriage could be contracted validly if the contracting parties knew that marriage was a perpetual and exclusive union instituted for the procreation of children, though there was not present any point of reference between their knowledge and the nature and mode of generation.[72] Gasparri required only a general notion of the essence of marriage, and no knowledge of the manner of generation. Ignorance of the mode of generation, namely, of the carnal union which must serve as the act for the begetting of children, did not preclude the possible presence of matrimonial consent, or, in consequence, the possible validity of marriage. A person who consented to a union for the procreation of children implicitly consented also to the right by the use of which, through carnal intercourse, the purpose of the union could be achieved.[73]

The Roman Rota accepted and followed the opinion of Gasparri. In a case reviewed in 1910 the Rota admitted that a general notion of the obligations inherent in marriage constituted a sufficient knowledge for the valid contraction of marriage,[74] and accordingly refused a declaration of nullity to a woman who

71 S. C. C., *in Ventimillien.*, 19 maii 1888 — *Thesaurus*, CXLVII (1888), 289, 518.

72 "Sufficit autem ut haec intelligere valeat in confuso, nempe illud consortium perpetuum et exclusivum instituendum esse in ordine ad filios procreandos, quin noverit ea quae spectant ad naturam modumque generationis." — Gasparri, *Tractatus Canonicus de Matrimonio* (3 ed., 2 vols., Parisiis, 1904), II, n. 881.

73 "Si puella nubens scit matrimonium esse societatem cum viro, qui ex uxore filios procreat, et in hanc societatem ad filios procreandos consentit, sed nescit filios haberi per carnalem copulam, imo hanc carnalem copulam prorsus ignorat, est causa ignorantiae, quae non excludit matrimonialem consensum et coniugii valorem, cum puella, consentiens in societatem ad filiorum procreationem, implicite consenserit in ipsum coeundi ius." — Gasparri, *ibidem*, n. 901.

74 S. R. R., *Nullitatis Matrimonii*, 17 mart. 1910, coram R. P. D. Iosepho Mori, dec. XII, n. 4: "Notio generalis circa matrimonialia munera per se sufficiens est, coeteris concurrentibus, ad matrimonium validum contrahendum." — *S. R. R. Decisiones*, II (1910), 117.

claimed that she had entered into marriage without any knowledge regarding carnal intercourse. The woman tried to convince the court that no valid consent was given, since she had intended to bind herself to nothing more than the performance of household duties. Subsequent investigation, however, revealed that the woman knew that it was through some act of the married couple that children were brought into their family.[75] The Rota, therefore, declared that the woman had sufficient knowledge to contract a valid marriage. It appealed to the opinion of Gasparri to show that she did not exclude any conjugal right, since the right to coition was implicitly contained in the consent given by her.[76] All that was required, according to the Rota, was a knowledge of the essence and of the end of marriage, which the woman evidently had.[77]

This decision of the Rota was the immediate forerunner to the law expressed in the present Code of Canon Law. It represented the ultimate development as found in the works of Cardinal Gasparri, who exerted such a notable influence in the codification of Canon Law. The Code could not but state that the contracting parties must at least know that marriage is a permanent society between man and woman for the procreation of children.[78]

75 " 'Sapeva che dalla magior parte dei matrimonii nascono fanciulli: sapeva che alcun atto deve procedere . . .' " — *S. R. R. Decisiones, ibidem,* p. 116, n. 3.

76 *S. R. R. Decisiones, ibidem,* p. 117, n. 4.

77 "[Constat] sufficientem adfuisse scientiam de substantia et fine essentiali matrimonii, ideoque non defuisse consensum ex parte contractus." — *S. R. R. Decisiones, ibidem,* p. 121, n. 10.

78 "Ut matrimonialis consensus haberi possit, necesse est ut contrahentes saltem non ignorent matrimonium esse societatem permanentem inter virum et mulierem ad filios procreandos." — Canon 1082, §1.

PART TWO

CANONICAL COMMENTARY

CHAPTER III

GENERAL NOTIONS

Matrimony, considered *"in fieri"* or actively, is a legitimate contract whereby a man and woman by their mutual consent give and accept the permanent and exclusive right to each other's body for the procreation and education of children. Considered *"in facto esse"* or passively, it is the union of a man and woman arising from this mutual consent.[1]

This twofold definition of matrimony offers a clear picture of the elements essential to a valid marriage. Thus matrimony contains all the elements essential to a true bilateral contract. A contract is the agreement of two or more parties on the same thing, involving an obligation arising from commutative justice incumbent upon each party of giving, doing, or omitting to do something. The elements of a contract, therefore, are: 1.) two or more persons; 2.) an object; 3.) a legitimate consent; 4.) a consideration; 5.) an obligation arising from commutative justice; 6.) and an obligation incumbent mutually upon each party.[2]

1 St. Thomas, *Summa Theologica,* diligenter emendata Nicolai, Sylvii, Billuart et C. J. Drioux notis ornata, 6. ed. (8 vols., Barri-Ducis, 1870), Suppl., q. 44, 2 ad 1; Sanchez, *De Sancto Matrimonii Sacramento,* lib. II, disp. 1, n. 1, ss; Schmalzgrueber, *Ius Ecclesiasticum Universum* (5 vols. in 12, Romae, 1843-1845), lib. IV, tit. I, n. 288; Cappello, *Tractatus Canonico-Moralis de Sacramentis* (3 vols. in 6, Vol. III, *De Matrimonio,* 4. ed., Taurini-Romae, 1939), Vol. III, Pars I, n. 2 (hereafter cited *De Matrimonio).*

2 Vermeersch, *Theologiae Moralis Principia, Responsa, Consilia* (editio tertia, 4 vols., Università Gregoriana, Romae; 1933-1937), Vol. II, nn. 374, 376 (hereafter cited Vermeersch, *Theologia Moralis); Cappello, De Matrimonio,* n. 23.

In every valid marriage there are: 1) two persons, a man and a woman; 2) the offer and the acceptance of the right to each other's body in a common conjugal life; 3) their mutual consent; 4) the proposed procreation and education of children, an acknowledged mutual aid, and the recognized remedy for concupiscence; 5) the assumed duty of a strict conjugal fidelity regarding the marital obligations inherent in the contract; and 6) the reciprocal nature of this duty or obligation as binding equally upon both parties.[3]

As a true contract, marriage is subject to the general rules governing contracts, and hence must contain the essential contractual elements, namely the matter of the contract and the consent by which it is effected. Otherwise there can be no true contract.[4] Moreover, these elements must be such as to constitute marriage in its own specific being, specifically determining the contract as a matrimonial contract. According to contractual law, every valid contract must be actuated by the deliberate consent of the contracting parties. The contracting parties must know what is essential to their agreement, and they must freely indicate their will to enter into such an agreement. In a valid marriage contract, therefore, a man and a woman must know what essentially pertains to marriage, and they must voluntarily agree to enter into a matrimonial union.

Since a matrimonial contract must be effected knowingly and freely, it is pertinent to indicate here what is essential to marriage, and what elements of marriage must be known and willed by the contracting parties if a valid marriage is to gain existence between them.

Article I — The Essential Object of Marriage

The first element to be considered is the object of the contract. What do a man and a woman intend when they agree to marry? What do they will to do? The essential object of

3 Cappello, *loc. cit.*

4 Vermeersch-Creusen, *op. cit.*, II, n. 376.

marriage is variously designated by authors as the marriage bond, the marriage union, the marital relationship and the conjugal right.[5] The Code dealing specifically with the knowledge necessary for the contracting of marriage, visualizes the essential object as a permanent and exclusive society between a man and a woman.[6] One should not be confused by such a variety of terms. Actually they all mean the same thing. A man and a woman when marrying intend to form a union, to create a bond between themselves, to effect an intimate mutual relationship by giving and accepting the right to each other's body,[7] all of which is to say that they intend to form a society as envisioned by the Code, for a society as such is simply a union of intelligent beings, bound by mutual rights and obligations, for the persecution of a common end.[8] The essential object of the matrimonial contract, therefore, is a conjugal society that has its foundation in the mutual concession and acceptance of corporal rights.

The intimate union willed by the parties in marriage seems to imply the necessity for cohabitation and the need of a community of bed and board, but such cohabitation and community do not pertain to the essence of the matrimonial contract. They are required rather for the integrity and perfection of conjugal life.[9] This is clearly deducible from the legislation of the Code which permits, for example, a marriage of conscience and legitimate separation.[10]

A distinction must likewise be drawn between the right that is granted and received in marriage on the one hand, and the

5 St. Thomas, *Summa Theologica*, Suppl., q. 44, art. 1; q. 49, art. 3; Barbosa, *Collectanea Doctorum tam Veterum quam Recentiorum in Ius Pontificium Universum* (5 vols., Lugduni, 1637), IV, I, n. 7; Payen, *De Matrimonio in Missionibus* (Zi-Ka-Wei, Typographia T'OU-SE-WE, 1935-1936), I, n. 75, ad fin.; Vlaming, *Praelectiones Iuris Matrimonii ad Normam Codicis Iuris Canonici* (3. ed., 2 vols., Bussum in Hollandia, 1919-1921), I, n. 15; Cappello, *op. cit.*, Vol. I, Pars I, n. 7.

6 Canon 1082, §1.

7 Payen, *op. cit.*, I, n. 70.

8 Macksey, *De Ethica Naturali* (Romae, 1914), p. 412 sq.

9 Cappello, *De Matrimonio*, n. 6.

10 Cf. canons 1104, 1128, 1129.

exercise of that right on the other. Only the right itself is essential to the marriage contract. A valid marriage pact can exist irrespective of the actual execution of conjugal acts Hincmar of Rheims (†882) in the ninth century designated the act of copulation as an essential element for the formation of a marriage.[11] Hincmar was followed in this opinion by Gratian,[12] and in general by the School of Bologna.

Ivo of Chartres (1040-1117) opposed the *copula* theory, as this opinion was called,[13] as St. Peter Damian (†1072) had done before him.[14] The principal opposition to the *copula* theory, however, came from Peter the Lombard († ca. 1160),[15] and the Parisian School. Peter and his followers held that the consent of the parties sufficed in itself to effect a true and perfect marriage, so much so that once consent was given, before any act of consummation, the marriage was indissoluble. Alexander III (1159-1181), who before his election to the pontificate was known as Rolandus Bandinelli, Magister of the School of Bologna, settled the question by decreeing that the consent alone was the efficient cause of marriage. However, he denied the absolute indissolubility of a non-consummated marriage.[16]

The distinction between a right and the exercise of a right is of maximum importance, for from it flows the solution of the principal problem of this treatise, namely, the question of the

11 *De Nuptiis Stephani et Filiae Regimundi Regis:* "Nec habeant in se Christi et Ecclesiae sacramentum, sicut beatus Augustinus dicit, si se nuptialiter non utuntur, id est, si eas non subsequitur commixtio sexuum." — Migne, *Patrologiae Cursus Completus, Series Latina* (221 vols., Parisiis, 1844-1864), CXXVI, 137 (hereafter cited *MPL);* Joyce, *Christian Marriage* (London and New York, 1933), pp. 54 ff.

12 "Sciendum est, quod coniugium desponsatione initiatur, commixtione perficitur; unde inter sponsum et sponsam coniugium est, sed initiatum; inter copulatos est coniugium ratum." — *Dictum Gratiani,* ad c. 34, C. XXVII, q. 2.

13 *Ep.* 246 — *MPL,* CLXII, 253.

14 *Opusc.* 41: *De Tempore Celebrandi Nuptiis* — *MPL,* CXLV, 660.

15 *Petrus Lombardus Libri IV Sententiarum* (2. ed., 2 vols., ad claras aquas ex typographis Collegii S. Bonaventurae, 1916), II, 917, 918, 921.

16 C. 4, X, *de sponsalibus et matrimoniis,* IV, 3.

necessity for the validity of a marriage contract of knowledge concerning carnal intercourse, which pertains to the exercise of the marital right. If the concession and acceptance of the right to conjugal relations alone pertain to the essence of matrimony, then ignorance regarding the matter of carnal intercourse, since it is reduced to a mere effect of the marriage contract.[17] does not affect the validity of the contract.

Article II. The Ends of Marriage

The ends of marriage, as set forth in canon 1013, §1, are the procreation and the education of children — the primary end; mutual aid and remedy for concupiscence — the secondary ends.[18]

Procreation is a familiar concept. It may be described here as the conception and birth of a child resulting from the intimate union of a man and a woman. It is a natural physical effect of the marital act. Education, the second element of the primary end, is a necessary obligation arising from the procreation of children. Man, since he is composed of a body and a rational soul, enjoys both a physical and a moral life. His physical life is provided for through generation; his moral life, which is to perfect him in his rational nature, is developed through education.[19] The parents, who are responsible for the physical life of the child, are obliged by virtue of their parenthood to provide for its religious and moral education, to make the child a healthy member of a civil society, and to furnish it with the necessary temporal goods.[20]

17 "Dicendum est consensum matrimonium constituentem non esse explicite in carnalem copulam sed in jus et potestatem ad talem copulam, quia carnalis copula non est de matrimonii essentia, sed ejus effectus et operatio." — Sanchez, *loc. cit.*

18 "Matrimonii finis primarius est procreatio atque educatio prolis; secundarius mutuum adiutorium et remedium concupiscientiae." — Canon 1013, §1.

19 Cappello, *De Matrimonio*, n. 8.

20 "Parentes gravissima obligatione tenentur prolis educationem tum religiosam et moralem, tum physicam et civilem pro viribus curandi, et etiam temporali eorum bono providendi." — canon 1113.

Mutual aid, a secondary end of marriage, implies principally the life-partnership in which the spouses spiritually, physically, psychologically and economically complement one another.[21] It generally includes the ideas of cohabitation, life in common, and conjugal society.[22]

The remedy for concupiscence, the third end of marriage, traces its origin to the fall of man.[23] Marriage in serving as a remedy for concupiscence is not to be understood in the sense that it extinguishes or even diminishes sexual desire. Nor does it mean that marriage eliminates the possibility of excess or perversion in sexual matters. The marriage contract is ordained as a remedy for concupiscence inasmuch as the matrimonial bond gives a legitimate scope to sexual desire and imposes the obligation of marital chastity, thereby acting as a restraining influence on the parties in their dealings with one another, and forbidding all indulgence outside their marital union.[24]

These three ends, the procreation and the education of children, mutual aid, and remedy for concupiscence, are the essential ends of matrimony although that is not explicitly so stated in the Code.[25]

They are essential not in the sense that marriage connot exist without their actual realization, — the marriage bond does

21 Ford, *The Validity of Virginal Marriage* (Worcester, Mass., Harrigan Press, 1938), p. 20.

22 Pius XI, litt. encycl., *Casti connubii,* 31 dec. 1930: "Matrimonium . . . latius ut totius vitae communio, consuetudo, societas accipiatur." — *Acta Apostolicae Sedis, Commentarium Officiale* (Romae, 1909 —), XXII (1930), 549 (hereafter cited *AAS*).

23 Cf. Noldin-Schmitt, *Summa Theologiae Moralis* (26 ed., 3 vols., Oeniponte-Lipsiae: Typis et Sumptibus Felician Rauch, 1938-1940), Vol. III, *De Sacramentis,* n. 504 (hereafter cited *De Sacramentis).*

24 Ford, *op. cit.,* p. 18.

25 That both the primary and the secondary ends mentioned in canon 1013, §1, are essential to the marriage contract is the common and traditional opinion of canonists and theologians. The usual doctrine is given by Wernz-Vidal, *Ius Canonicum* (7 vols. in 8, Romae: Apud Aedes Universitatis Gregorianae, 1927-1938), Vol. V, *Ius Matrimoniale* (2. ed., 1928), n. 26 (hereafter cited *Ius Matrimoniale).*

not cease to exist when, for example, sterility precludes the possibility of procreation; nor is the bond dissolved when acts of mutual aid cease, as in the case of separation from bed and board — but rather because of their essential relationship to the matter of the marriage contract.[26] The parties in marrying may have any number of purposes or motives in view when they make the contract. But marriage itself, the object of their consent, cannot exist without being objectively ordered to these three ends. The marriage bond always involves the right to marital intercourse. However, the procreation and the education of children, the enjoyment of a mutual aid, and the remedy for concupiscence are realized by the exercise of the marital right.

Canon 1013, § 1, as previously noted, makes a distinction between the primary and secondary ends. This distinction is based on the fundamental nature of the procreation and the education of children. There is no degree of difference in the essential character of the ends. One may not say that the primary end of marriage is more essential than the secondary ends. All three ends are equally essential. But the procreation and the education of children necessarily include to a certain extent respectively the remedy for concupiscence and the factor of a mutual aid, which conversely is not true. The remedy for concupiscence is included in the marriage act by which procreation is realized, and the necessity for mutual aid is involved in the obligation of educating the offspring.[27]

The distinction is worthy of note, for canon 1082, § 1, the subject of this treatise, states that it suffices for a valid marriage that the contracting parties know that marriage is a permanent society for the procreation of children.[28] The canon would not be adequate, inasmuch as the factor of mutual aid and the

26 Cf. Wernz-Vidal, *loc. cit.*, Cappello, *De Matrimonio*, n. 9.

27 C. St. Thomas, *Summa Theologica, Supplementum*, q. 49, art. 2, ad 1; Palmieri, *Tractatus de Matrimonio* (Romae: Typis Polyglottis, 1880), thes. 2, n. V; Vermeersch, *Theologia Moralis*, IV, n. 41.

28 "Ut matrimonialis consensus haberi possit, necesse est ut contrahentes saltem non ignorent matrimonium esse societatem permanentem inter virum et mulierem ad filios procreandos."

remedy for concupiscence are essential ends of marriage, if the secondary ends were not necessarily included in the primary end, the procreation of children as mentioned in the canon.

Besides the essential ends there may be numerous accidental ends influencing the actuation of a marriage contract. These accidental ends, such as family honor, riches, peace, etc., have no bearing on the question of this study. Only the essential elements of marriage are involved here, for only the essential elements can affect the validity of the marriage.

Article III — The Properties of Marriage

Not only in relation to the object and the ends of marriage, but also with reference to the properties of marriage an essential note is predicable. Marriage is essentially one and indissoluble.[29]

Unity in marriage militates against the simultaneous existence of more than one matrimonial bond. Marriage must be contracted between one man and one woman; a man or a woman cannot enter into a new matrimonial contract as long as he or she is bound by a previous marital bond.[30]

Specifically opposed to the unity of the marriage contract are simultaneous polyandry and polygyny. Polyandry designates the union of one woman with two or more men. Such a union is contrary to the primary precepts of the natural law. It gives woman the dominant position in society, and destroys her natural subjugation to man.[31] Polyandry is likewise opposed to the primary end of marriage inasmuch as the proper education of a child cannot be secured when the paternity of that child is uncertain — a situation which certainly arises in polyandrous marriage.[32] Simultaneous polygyny contemplates the marital

29 Cf. canon 1013, §2.

30 Gasparri, *Tractatus Canonicus de Matrimonio,* I, n. 10; Cappello, *De Matrimonio,* n. 16.

31 Cf. Vermeersch-Creusen, *Epitome Iuris Canonici,* II (5. ed., Mechliniae-Romae, 1934), n. 275.

32 Cf. Vermeersch-Creusen, *loc. cit.*

union of one man with two or more women. It renders at least difficult the attainment of the secondary ends of marriage, and is prohibited by the divine law.[33]

Indissolubility makes of marriage a perpetual union inviolable by any merely human authority.[34] It is opposed to divorce, whether the divorce contemplated be perfect or imperfect. Perfect divorce has as its object the dissolution of the bond itself with the consequent right of each party to marry again if he or she so chooses. Indissolubility in relation to this type of divorce is not to be taken in an exclusively absolute sense. Its force is regulated rather by the type of marriage to which it is applied. The bond of a legitimate marriage may be dissolved by virtue of the Pauline privilege.[35] A non-consummated sacramental marriage may become subjected to its perfect dissolution by reason of a solemn religious profession or through a dispensation granted by the Apostolic See.[36] A consummated sacramental marriage alone remains absolutely indissoluble.[37]

Imperfect divorce relieves the parties of the obligation of conjugal society, or, more commonly, consists in a separation from bed and board. It does not include the dissolution of the marital bond. The marital bond remains intact, and prevents the parties from entering into a new marriage contract.[38] Imperfect divorce may become applicable in any type of marriage. A legitimate separation may be obtained by the innocent party for a grave reason, for example, when an act of

33 Monogamy is the original form of marriage as found in the garden of Paradise. Polygamy was permitted to the patriarchs in the Old Testament, but with the New Covenant our Divine Saviour restored marriage to its original form, and made the bond essentially one and exclusive. — Matt., XIX, 3-9; Mark, X, 1-12; St. Thomas, *Summa Theologica, Suppl.*, q. 65, art. 1, ad 7; Innocent III, in c. 8, X, *de divortiis*, IV, 19.

34 Cf. Vermeersch-Creusen, *loc. cit.*

35 Cf. canon 1120, §1.

36 Cf. canon 1119.

37 Cf. Canon 1118.

38 Cf. Prümmer, *Manuale Theologiae Moralis*, III (4.-5. ed., Friburgi Brisgoviae: Herder & Co., 1928), p. 475.

adultery, or the neglect of the Catholic education of the offspring, etc., attach to the other party in the union.[39]

The possibility of a dissolution or of a separation does not detract from the essential character of indissolubility in marriage. Those who wish to contract marriage must necessarily consent to the concession of a mutually permanent and exclusive right, and to the exercise of a communal life.[40] If the right granted is not both permanent and exclusive, then the consent is not a true matrimonial consent, and a valid marriage does not exist.

Article IV. The Efficient Cause of the Marriage Contract

After a consideration of the object, the ends and the properties of marriage, it is in order to turn now to an investigation of its efficient cause. According to canon 1081, § 1, marriage is effected by the consent of the contracting parties.[41] The efficient causality of consent was recognized early in the history of matrimonial legislation. Ulpian, the Roman jurist, insisted on consent as the constituent element of marriage.[42] His opinion was accepted and given legal force by incorporation into the *Corpus Iuris Civilis of Justinian.*[43]

Ecclesiastical authority gave the dictum of Ulpian a new meaning, declaring that consent was the exclusive cause of the marriage contract. Independent of the actual exercise of the exchanged right, or of the realization of the ends of marriage,

39 Cf. canons 1129, §1; 1131, §1.

40 Cf. canons 1081, §2; 1128.

41 "Matrimonium facit partium consensus inter personas iure habiles legitime manifestatus; qui nulla humana potestate suppleri valet."

42 "Nuptias non concubitus sed consensus facit." — Ulpianus, *in XXXVI ad Sabinum*, D. (50, 17), 30.

43 According to Roman Law, marriage consisted in the "affectio maritalis," that is, in the will to be husband and wife in conjunction with an actual cohabitation. There was no matrimonial consent as we understand it now. — Cf. Vignali, *Corpo del Diritto, corredato delle note di Dionisio Golofredo di C. E. Freiesleben, altrimento Ferromontano* (8 vols., Napoli, 1859), *Digesto*, VI, 1202.

the consent of the parties sufficed to perfect the contract and to effect the marital union. Thus Pope Nicholas I (858-867) in a response to the Bulgarians decreed that simply the consent of the parties sufficed to constitute marriage.[44]

Three centuries later the same thought was expressed almost verbatim by Pope Innocent III (1198-1216). To a question concerning the eligibility of deaf-mutes for the contracting of marriage Innocent replied in the affirmative, because, as he said, consent alone was necessary for marriage.[45] Further confirmation was given to the principle in Constitutions by Eugene IV (1431-1437) and Urban VIII (1623-1644).[46]

Consent in itself is an act of the will. Taking consent as the efficient cause of marriage, and putting together the essential elements of matrimony thus far gathered, one will note that matrimonial consent is an act of the will whereby both parties to marriage give and accept the perpetual and exclusive right to each other's body, the specific object being those acts which of themselves are ordained for the generation of children.[47] Now, the will is a blind faculty which requires illumination from the intellect. The intellect must indicate to the will the object of its activity and the reason why it acts. A person wishing to marry, therefore, must first know what is essential to the marriage contract. The will acts upon the knowledge presented by the intellect and thus the marriage contract is effected.

44 Cf. C. 2, C. XXVII, q. 2 — Jaffé, n. 2812.

45 "Sufficiat ad matrimonium solus consensus illorum de quorum quarumque coniunctionibus agitur." — C. 23, X, *de sponsalibus et matrimonio*, IV, 1. — Potthast, n. 329.

46 Eugenius IV, const. *Exultate Deo*, 22 nov. 1439: "Septimum est sacramentum matrimonii. . . . Causa efficiens matrimonii regulariter est mutuus consensus per verba de pesenti expressus." — *Bullarum Diplomatum et Privilegiorum Sanctorum Romanorum Pontificum Tauriensis Editio* (24 Vols. et 2 Appendices, Augustae Taurinorum, Neapoli, 1857-1885), V. 51 (hereafter cited Bullarium); Urbanus VIII, Const. *Magnum in Christo*, 20 iun. 1637: "Magnum in Christo et in Ecclesia matrimonii sacramentum, ut vitae est legitima inter virum et feminam indissolubilis societas, in qua ex pari consensu semetipsum alter alteri debet." — *op. cit.*, XIV, 595.

47 Cf. canon 1081, §2.

A. *Qualities of a Valid Matrimonial Consent*

Matrimonial consent must be endowed with those qualities that are generally required for the institution of any valid bilateral contract. It must be true, deliberate, mutual, externally manifested by competent persons.[48] The qualities of mutuality and manifestation have no connection with the subject of this study, and need only to be mentioned here. Here the concern of the writer involves principally the deliberation necessary and, in a relative way, the character of the true consent.

The matrimonial consent must be deliberate, that is, it must be placed with the full advertence of the mind and executed with a perfect act of the will. In giving his consent a person must know first of all the object of his consent, namely that to which he consents, for no one wills that which he does not know. His consent, too, must be an act of his own will, freely given. This quality of deliberateness in the matrimonial consent is opposed to ignorance and error, to force and to fear. Again, the consent must be a true consent, that is, the external expression of the contracting parties must reflect a true internal intention. For example, when a person states that he wills to contract marriage, he must truly will to enter marriage. To simulate consent by externally indicating a will to enter marriage while internally there is the opposite intention of not contracting marriage, or of not taking upon oneself the conjugal obligations, or of not acknowledging the duty of fulfilling these obligations, is to destroy the validity of the contract. Persons who would thus express consent would act like children at play who go through the formality of contracting marriage without knowing what marriage is, and therefore without intending to form a marital union.

With deliberation as a necessary quality of consent a real foundation is established for the analysis of ignorance as a hindrance to the formation of a valid marriage. For ignorance,

48 Sanchez, *op. cit.*, lib. IV, disp. 10, n. 2, disp. 28, n. 1, disp. 32, n. 1; Schmalzgrueber, *ibidem*, nn. 246, 264; Pirhing, *Ius Canonicum Nova Methodo Explicatum*, lib. IV, tit. I, nn. 82.

inasmuch as it impedes consent, thereby impedes also the effect of consent, which in this case is the matrimonial contract.

B. *Ignorance*

Ignorance may be defined as the privation of knowledge in a subject naturally capable of and constituted for knowledge.[49] It is vincible or invincible in so far as it can or cannot be overcome through the use of moral diligence. Vincible ignorance, moreover, is an affected ignorance if it is directly willed; crass, supine, or simple, if it flows from crass, supine or simple negligence.

Since the definition speaks only of a subject capable of acquiring knowledge, insane persons and infants, in view of their intellectual inability, as well as those who act under the influence of intoxicating drink and passion, are improperly said to be ignorant. However, in order to show the necessity for knowledge in the contracting of marriage such subjects may also be considered, since their inability to give consent is founded on their lack of knowledge, i.e., they are in ignorance under these particular conditions.

To prepare for a clear analysis of the relation of ignorance to marriage, the following division of ignorance is offered, namely, subsistent ignorance, which is ignorance according to the strict terms of the definition, and contingent ignorance which results from a state of mind in which mental activity is impossible or at least impaired. In accordance with this division one may more easily classify the subjects affected by ignorance and measure the effect which it has on their matrimonial consent.

Contingent ignorance may with reference to its object be divided into absolute and relative ignorance. Absolute ignorance denotes a condition brought about by a total lack of the use of reason. One who is deprived of the use of reason is incapable of acquiring any rational knowledge, and as a result is ignorant of anything and everything. Relative ignorance on the other hand is understood to indicate a lack of some particular

49 St. Thomas, *Summa Theologica*, Ia-IIae, q. 76, art. 2.

knowledge. The object of such ignorance is confined to specific concepts. A person may be capable of some intellectual activity, but not to such an extent that he may comprehend what is meant by a marriage contract, that is, the knowledge which he has acquired may not be proportionate to that demanded in the execution of a valid marriage contract.

Relative ignorance, in so far as it is opposed to matrimonial consent, has as its object the essential elements of marriage, that fact of marriage, or both. By the fact of marriage is meant the very act by which the marriage contract is brought into being. For example, if a person has habitual knowledge of what matrimony is, that is, if he enjoys a complete understanding of the essential elements of marriage and the manner in which marriage is contracted, but does not know that he is here and now contracting marriage, he is said to be ignorant of the fact of marriage and therefore not validly married.

Upon presentation of these general notions of the nature of marriage, of its efficient causality, and of the effects of ignorance on consent, it is in order to pass to a consideration of the canon law regarding ignorance as affecting the matrimonial consent.

CHAPTER IV

CONTINGENT IGNORANCE

Canon 1082, § 1, states that for a valid marriage it is necessary that the contracting parties be not ignorant of the fact that marriage is a permanent society between a man and a woman for the procreation of children. Knowledge, then, is by law a prerequisite for the act of instituting a valid marriage contract. Without due deliberation and discretion a marital union cannot be perfected. It follows from this that if a person is so afflicted that in him mental activity is impossible, or at least impaired to such an extent that he is unable to understand the significance of marriage, or incapable of the deliberation required for the placing of a voluntary act whereby the contract is efected, he cannot validly marry. The inability of such a person to contract marriage is founded on his inability to elicit a valid matrimonial consent, which in turn is precluded by reason of contingent ignorance. The lack of mental activity or the defect thereof interferes with the acquisition of that knowledge in respect of marriage without which a true matrimonial consent cannot be given.

Contingent ignorance, resulting from an impaired mental activity, or from a complete lack thereof, may be attributed to a cause which is either subsistent and permanent, or incidental and temporary.

Article I. Subsistent Causes of Contingent Ignorance

A subsistent cause of contingent ignorance is understood to mean a permanent cause of a continued state of ignorance. It finds its exemplification in a mental or physical defect which renders a person incapable of acquiring knowledge of the essence of marriage and therefore incapable also of eliciting a valid matrimonial consent.

A. Mental Defects

A mental defect interferes with the operation of the intellectual faculty or renders its operation impossible. If a mental defect so impedes the operation of the intellectual faculty that a person is unable to grasp the significance of marriage, then that mental defect is to be considered a subsistent cause of a state of ignorance. A person made ignorant by such a mental defect, moreover, cannot validly marry, for he lacks even the minimum knowledge that is required by canon 1082, § 1.[1]

(a) *Insanity*

Insanity is a mental defect through which a person is deprived of the use of reason, and therefore is made incapable of acquiring knowledge. The inability to acquire knowledge in turn militates against the giving of a valid matrimonial consent, for consent is essentially an act of the will, and one does not will what one does not know.[2] Supervenient insanity has no effect upon a marriage already established as a fact. A marriage once contracted by persons of sound mind remains a valid marriage in that it was established as a permanent union, even though upon the formation of the contract one or both of the parties become insane.[3] There is no incompatible opposition between an existing marriage bond and a supervening mental affliction; they may and do exist simultaneously. An abnormal mental state, therefore, does not of itself offer any sufficient reason for the dissolution of a marriage bond. The bond remains intact, even though the mental affliction renders impossible the fulfillment of the marital obligations. Insanity rather interferes with the actuation of a marriage bond. It is directly opposed to the eliciting of

1 "Ut matrimonialis consensus haberi possit, necesse est ut contrahentes saltem non ignorent matrimonium esse societatem permanentem inter virum et mulierem ad filios procreandos."

2 St. Thomas, *Summa Theologica, Suppl.*, q. 58, art. 3.

3 C. 26, C. XXXII, q. 7. — Jaffé, n. 80; Gasparri, *Tractatus Canonicus de Matrimonio*, II, 12; Gougnard, *Tractatus de Matrimonio* (7. ed., Mechliniae, H. Dessain, 1931), p. 150.

matrimonial consent,[4] and in consequence to the establishing of a marriage contract.

Since insanity is directly opposed to the eliciting of matrimonial consent, it is evident that it affects the validity of marriage only when it is concomitant with the formation of the marriage contract.[5] When the state of insanity exists prior or subsequent to the moment in which the consent is given by the contracting parties, the marriage may not be declared invalid on the ground of insanity. For if at the time when the consent is given the parties are in possession of their faculties, and actually will to contract marriage, their consent is valid, and the bond resulting from their consent is a true matrimonial bond. In practice therefore, to establish that a marriage is invalid because of insanity, it is necessary to prove the existence of insanity and its impact on the contract.

Given the necessity of the existence of insanity at the moment of the outward exchange of consent, it may be stated that isolated acts of insanity are not presumed to impede the contracting of marriage unless they are directly related to the act whereby the outward manifestation of consent is effected.[6] Furthermore, if a deranged person enjoys lucid moments during which he has the use of reason and the necessary knowledge, he can at such moments exchange a consent wherewith he contracts a valid marriage.[7]

A lucid interval envisions a considerable period of time in which all the actions and words of a mentally defective person conform to the rules of prudence.[8] It is not to be confused with complete recovery from a mental disorder, or with a latent period during which only the external manifestation of insanity is lacking. Very often a mentally deranged person reacts to suggestions or performs actions as deriving simply from the

4 St. Thomas, *loc. cit.*

5 Gougnard, *op. cit.*, p. 150.

6 S. R. R., *Nullitatis Matrimonii,* 1 mart. 1930, coram R. P. D. Arcturo Wynen, dec. XII, n. 9 — *S. R. R. Decisiones,* XXII (1930), 131.

7 Covarrubias, *Opera Omnia,* pars II, c. II, n. 6; Sanchez, *op. cit.*, lib. I, disp. VIII, n. 17; Pirhing, *Jus Canonicum,* lib. IV, tit. I, sec. I, n. 10.

8 Pallottini, s. v. *Matrimonium,* III, *Quoad consensum,* n. 12.

habits of his daily life. These actions are not to be construed as indicative of a lucid interval. Suggested and habitual actions are almost automatic actions; they do not prerequire any considerable measure of sanity. They differ greatly from actions which proceed from deliberate decisions.[9]

Many modern psychiatrists, as Gasparri says, deny the existence of intermediate periods of sanity, particularly when insanity is a congenital condition of the mind. They interpret these intervals simply as periods of mental quiescence, and accordingly deny the interpolated existence of the use of reason.[10] However, ecclesiastical jurisprudence still recognizes the possible existence of such intervals, and hence makes provision for determining the validity of marriages contracted during intermittent periods of sanity.

According to the unanimous opinion of both ancient and modern authors a marriage contracted during an intermediate period of sanity is a valid marriage. The obstacle resulting from the lack of the use of reason is no longer present, and a valid consent may be given.[11] But if a doubt arises regarding the validity of a marriage contracted at such a time, the contract is presumed to be invalid on the ground of defective consent, especially if the celebration of the marriage is preceded or followed by manifestly inordinate acts.[12]

Sanchez gives the reason for this presumption. He states that insanity is by nature perpetual and incurable, whereas lucid intervals are of a casual and aventitious character.[13] Conse-

[9] S. R. R., *Nullitatis Matrimonii,* 1 mart. 1930, coram R. P. D. Arcturo Wynen, dec. XII, n. 11 — *S. R. R. Decisiones,* XXII (1930), 133; S. R. R., *Nullitatis Matrimonii,* 27 aug. 1922, coram Rmo. P. D. Ioanne Prior, Decano, dec. XXXIX, n. 12 — *S. R. R. Decisiones,* XIV (1922), 320.

[10] Gasparri, *Tractatus Canonicus de Matrimonio,* II, 11.

[11] Covarrubias, *loc. cit.;* Sanchez, *loc. cit.;* Pirhing, *loc. cit.;* Gasparri, *loc. cit.;* Vlaming, *Praelectiones Iuris Matrimonii,* II, n. 519; Gougnard, *op. cit.,* p. 150.

[12] Vlaming, *loc. cit.;* Chelodi, *Ius Matrimoniale iuxta Codicem Iuris Canonici* (3. ed., Tridenti, 1921), n. 109.

[13] Sanchez, *op. cit.,* lib. I, disp. VIII, n. 17.

quently the state of insanity, once admitted as present, is presumed to prevail until the contrary is proved, and the acts performed are presumed to be invalid until a consideration of the quality of the acts and of the circumstances surrounding them furnishes proof which precludes this presumption.[14]

The presumption which points to the presence of insanity and to the consequent invalidity of the marriage does not seem to hold if the lucid intervals are very frequent. If the intermittent periods of sanity are so frequent that they displace insanity as the habitual state of the mind, and thus point to insanity as a casual condition, then very conclusive proof of the effect of insanity on the matrimonial consent must be produced before the contract can be declared invalid.[15]

Although a marriage contracted during a temporary period of sanity be valid, nevertheless the contracting of a marriage during such an interval must generally be considered to be illicit.[16] When a marriage is contracted under such circumstances there is no guarantee of immunity from recurring insanity or from the evil effects emanating therefrom. In particular, provision for the proper education of children is placed in jeopardy.[17] The proper care for the children is the responsibility of both parents, and the co-operation of both is required that their proper education may be secured. Co-operation is not assured when one of the parties to a marriage is mentally unsound.

For a grave reason a person may licitly marry while enjoying a lucid interval, for example, for the sake of gaining legitimate status for the children, or of obtaining a validated status for an already contracted civil marriage. Moreover, such a marriage may be more readily permitted if the man is the afflicted party. When the woman is the person defective there is greater danger

14 Pallottini, *ibidem*, n. 10; Gasparri, *op. cit.*, II, 11.

15 Pallottini, *ibidem*, n. 14.

16 Sanchez, *op. cit.*, lib. I, disp. VIII, n. 18; Schmalzgrueber, *Jus Ecclesiasticum Universum*, lib. IV, tit. I, n. 14.

17 Gasparri, *op. cit.*, II, 11; Gougnard, *op. cit.*, p. 150.

of injury to a child at conception and birth. If both parties are mentally unbalanced, they may never licitly marry.[18]

It is evident from what has already been said that insanity, engendering as it does the loss of the use of reason, constitutes a hindrance to marriage. But diseases of the mind, like diseases of the body, in general do not immediately appear in their completely evolved state. Rather, there is a gradual deterioration under which the mind, little by little, loses the use of reason. During the process of deterioration, until the mind has reached the state of complete and perfect insanity, the use of reason, however slight, is still present.[19] It is necessary, therefore, to determine to what degree the malady must have progressed before it can be maintained that a person has lost the power of deliberation which is necessary for the eliciting of a valid consent.

Perfect insanity, consisting of the complete loss of the use of reason, must be unequivocally acknowledged as an obstacle to the possible exchange of a matrimonial consent. Its influence is exercised and its effect is revealed in each and every action of the deranged person.[20] It precludes the possibility of any valid exchange of consent. A marriage contracted while such a state prevails is evidently invalid. But in the early stages of insanity, when only a few acts foreign to a sound mind are occasionally performed, one is not presumed to have lost the necessary faculty of deliberation requisite for a valid matrimonial consent.[21] On the other hand, in the very advanced stages of the malady the rational knowledge which underlies the acts performed is not such that these acts can be accepted or called the proper acts of the individual. Where is the line of demarcation to be drawn? As a general principle it may be stated that one who is capable of the degree of deliberation postulated for the commission of mortal

18 Gougnard, *loc. cit.*

19 Lehmkuhl, *Theologia Moralis* (5. ed., 2 vols., Friburgi Brisgoviae, 1888), II, n. 1090.

20 D'Annibale, *Summula Theologiae Moralis* (5. ed., 3 vols., Romae, 1908), I, n. 31.

21 S. R. R., *Nullitatis Matrimonii,* 1 mart. 1930, coram R. P. D. Arcturo Wynen, dec. XII, n. 7 — *S. R. R. Decisiones,* XXII (1930), 131.

sin is likewise endowed with the requisite mental capacity for the contracting of marriage.[22]

In the light of this applied principle it is not implied that anyone who is capable of committing any mortal sin must be judged to be capable also of eliciting a valid matrimonial consent. The ability of a person to perform an act is dependent upon the discretion of the person, which in itself must be proportionate to the act performed.[23] The eliciting of a matrimonial consent, having as its object the complex concept of marriage, requires a greater maturity of judgment and discretion than does the commission of a simple mortal sin.[24]

Thus anyone who has reached the age of reason may be deemed capable of committing a mortal sin, whereas the possession of the use of reason alone is hardly an indication that a person has the requisite mental capacity to give consent for marriage. For this reason the principle here proposed cannot simply be concerned with the discretion which involves a maturity of judgment and of knowledge pertinent to marriage, but must furthermore be concerned with the fuller deliberation which implies a sufficiently mature judgment and knowledge pertinent to the act whereby the matrimonial consent is given. In the application of this principle it is presupposed that the parties had, while of sound mind, a degree of discretion which sufficed for the valid contracting of marriage. The gradual deterioration of the mind wrought by progressive insanity then has its effect on the discretion that is proportionate to the consideration of

22 Sanchez, *De Sancto Matrimonii Sacramento,* lib. I, disp. VIII, n. 15; Reiffenstuel, *Ius Canonicum Universum,* lib. IV, tit. I, n. II; *S. R. R. Decisiones, ibidem,* n. 8.

23 S. R. R., *Nullitatis Matrimonii,* 28 aug. 1911, coram R. P. D. Aloysio Sincero, dec. XXXIX, n. 42 — *S. R. R. Decisiones,* III (1911), 450.

24 St. Thomas, *In 4 Libros Sententiarum,* Lib. IV, dist. 27, q. 2, art. 2, ad 2um: "Ad peccandum mortaliter sufficit etiam consensus praesens, sed in sponsalibus est consensus in futurum; major autem rationis discretio requiritur ad providendum in futurum, quam ad consentiendum in unum praesentem actum; et ideo ante potest homo peccare mortaliter, quam possit se obligare ad aliquid futurum." — *Opera Omnia,* studio ac labore Stanislai Frette et Pauli Mare (34 vols., Parisiis: Apud L. Vives, 1871-1880).

the concept of marriage, and not simply in relation to the possible commission of a mortal sin. Therefore, according to the norm given, if the state of the mind allows of a deliberation which is founded on a discretion proportionate to the concept of marriage, in the same degree that is required for the commission of a mortal sin, when the deliberation is founded on a discretion proportionate to the possible commission of the sin, then the mentally afflicted person must be deemed capable of eliciting a valid matrimonial consent.[25]

The norm has no value if progressive insanity has begun to take control of the mind before a person reached the age of puberty, or before he acquired a suffifficient knowledge of the nature of marriage; for in that case insanity becomes a barrier not only to the deliberation necessary for the giving of a valid matrimonial consent, but also to the fundamental understanding of what marriage is, that is, to the acquisition of a sufficient discretion for inaugurating a marriage contract. The interplay of ideas through which the necessary discretion for the possible contracting of marriage must be acquired[26] is itself inordinate. The case presents, therefore, a twofold defect, namely, in relation to the discretion required or understanding the nature of marriage, and consequently in relation also to the deliberation necessary for executing the act of consent. There is lacking the proportionate discretion and deliberation that is exemplified in the previous case in which the mentally defective person enjoyed

[25] Cappello *(De Matrimonio*, n. 579) and Doheny *(Canonical Procedure in Matrimonial Cases* [Milwaukee: The Bruce Publishing Company, 1938], p. 512) deny the efficacy of the principle. They argue that a greater amount of discretion is required for the instituting of a marriage contract than for the committing of a mortal sin. By the same reasoning it may be said that a greater amount of discretion is required for the commission of one sin than for the commission of another. But the relative discretion of a person in marrying or in committing a mortal sin is not in question; the norm is concerned rather with a common degree of deliberation founded on a discretion which is in diverse proportion with reference to the instituting of a marriage contract and to the committing of a mortal sin.

[26] Hickey, *Summula Philosophiae Scholasticae,* I (8. ed., St. Louis: Herder, 1933), n. 58.

at one time the mental capacity for the valid contracting of marriage.

Since the degree of deliberation required for the commission of mortal sin cannot be used as a criterion for determining in this instance the degree of insanity that invalidates the matrimonial consent, it is necessary, in any judgment regarding the ability or inability of a person for contracting marriage, to conduct a careful study of each case, with careful attention to the discretion of the parties and the deliberate character of the act of consent.

What has been said of progressive insanity may be applied also to the case of semi-insanity (stabilized imperfect state of insanity). If the permanent state of insanity permits that degree of deliberation which is postulated for the committing of a mortal sin, then the semi-insane person, if he had a sufficient discretion for the contracting of marriage before the condition of insanity appeared, can furnish a valid consent and enter into a matrimonial union. Without the previous existence of that sufficient discretion, however, there is little likelihood that the parties will be endowed with the requisite mental capactiy of exchanging a true matrimonial consent.

It has been seen that, with reference to the time and the degree in which it exists, insanity has an important bearing on the validity of matrimonial consent. In so far as insanity is coincident with the time when the contract is formed, and has progressed to such a degree as to prohibit the necssary deliberation it is an obstacle to the giving of matrimonial consent, and in consequence contracting of marriage. It is in the light of these two elements — time and degree — that there is reflected whatever indicates the character of the consent. It matters not what the cause of the insanity may be, or what form the insanity may take. Insanity essentially consists in an irrational state of the mind, and when that state exists at a prohibitive time and in a prohibitive degree, regardless of the cause or the classification of the insanity, the formation of a marriage contract becomes impossible. The cases adjudged by the Roman Rota give evidence of this fact. Whether insanity resulted, for example, from heredity, from a nervous collapse, or from a blow on the head; or whether it was classified as a case of dementia praecox, of paranoia, of traumatic psychosis, or of monomania, the effect was the same. The marriage had to be declared invalid on the ground of defective consent.[27]

(b) *Mental Deficiency*

Mental deficiency represents that phase of contingent ignorance in which ignorance is ultimately attributed to the lack of mental development. It is directly opposed to the acquisition of knowledge, and, therefore, to the performance of a voluntary act. The mentally deficient are generally classified — in accordance with an ascending degree of intelligence — as idiots, imbeciles, and morons. Idiocy reflects the lowest form of mental development. It results from a pathological process which affects the brain and its envelopes by retarding, arresting, or limiting the development of psychical functions, and originates either during intra-uterine life, or at the time of birth, or shortly afterwards.[28] In general, the mental ability of an idiot does not exceed that of a three year old child.

The inability of an idiot to contract marriage is immediately evident. Idiots never acquire the use of reason, and therefore are incapable of making any judgment involving abstract ideas. Without the rational faculty they can neither understand the nature of marriage nor give a consent that is based on such knowledge. But before a person can validly marry he must make

[27] S. R. R., *Nullitatis Matrimonii,* 9 apr. 1910, coram R. P. D. Gulielmo Sebastianelli, dec. XV, n. 2 — *S. R. R. Decisiones,* II (1910), 145; S. R. R., *Nullitatis Matrimonii,* 10 iul. 1909, coram R. P. D. Ioanne Prior, dec. X, n. 1 — *S. R. R. Decisiones,* I (1909), 86; S. R. R., *Nullitatis Matrimonii,* 15 maii 1915, coram R. P. D. Ioanne Prior, dec. XX, n. 1 — *S. R. R. Decisiones,* VII (1915), 216; S. R. R., *Nullitatis Matrimonii,* 27 aug. 1922, coram Rmo. P. D. Ioanne Prior, Decano, dec. XXXIX, n. 6 — *S. R. R. Decisiones,* XIV (1922), 315; S. R. R., *Nullitatis Matrimonii,* 7 apr. 1926, coram R. P. D. Iulio Grazioli, dec. XIV, n. 1 — *S. R. R. Decisiones,* XVIII (1926), 109.

[28] Dorcus-Shaffer, *Textbook of Abnormal Psychology* (1 ed., Williams & Wilkins: Baltimore, 1934), p. 293.

a judgment relative to the nature and essence of marriage, and must apply the knowledge acquired through that judgment in the deliberate act whereby the matrimonial consent is given.[29] Since such a judgment is beyond the capability of an idiot, the consent and the contract which depend on the previous act of judgment cannot exist.

Imbecility represents a higher degree of intelligence than idiocy. The mental development of the imbecile exceeds that of an idiot, but the mental age generally remains between three and seven years. Usually imbeciles are incapable of directing their own lives or of managing their own affairs with ordinary prudence, although with instruction they may sometimes attain a fairly high degree of proficiency in certain things.[30]

The possibility for an imbecile to elicit a valid matrimonial consent is very remote. His actions may give evidence of some rational activity, and the physiological experiences coincident with the age of puberty may create in the undeveloped mind an indication of the relationship between man and woman; however, it is highly improbable that a person so afflicted would enjoy such a facility with regard to intellectual activity that he could comprehend the manifold notes contained in a concept so complex as the marriage contract. The mere use of reason, even when perfectly normal, is no guarantee that a person has sufficient knowledge for the contracting of marriage. Over and above the use of reason there must be added a discretion which in its relation is proportionate to the marriage contract, so that a person actually knows what marriage is.[31]

Moreover, although the physical sensations incident to the attainment of puberty, inasmuch as they give meaning to the

29 Cf. canon 1082, §1.

30 Murray, *Introductory Sociology* (New York, 1936), p. 217; Dorcus-Shaffer, *op. cit.*, p. 296.

31 S. R. R., *Nullitatis Matrimonii*, 28 aug. 1911, coram Aloysio Sincero, dec. XXXIX, n. 42 — "Discretio addit supra usum rationis maturitatem iudicii contractui celebrando, idest, in casu nostro, matrimonio, proportionatum, ita ut contrahens naturam et vim contractus, seu, in casu nostro, quid sit matrimonium, eiusdemque essentiales proprietates, sat intelligere valeat saltem in confuso." — *S. R. R. Decisiones*, III (1911), 450.

corporal right that is transferred through the marriage contract, contribute to the knowledge required for the giving of a matrimonial consent, they are relevant to matrimonial consent only in so far as the intellect is able to associate them with the object and the ends of marriage. A great deal of intellectual activity, therefore, is demanded for the production of the knowledge postulated for the exchange of a valid matrimonial consent. Since an imbecile is incapable of such activity, he cannot furnish a valid consent for marriage. The Roman Rota granted a declaration of nullity when it was proved that a man was unable to cultivate his land, could not distinguish his property from other peoples' goods, did not realize that he was the husband of the girl he married, and consequently did not protest the adultery openly committed by his reputed wife. [32] The Rota decided in view of these circumstances that the mental deficiency precluded the very possibility of the exchange of a valid consent for his marriage.

A moron may be described as a person having a mental age ranging from eight to twelve years. He is capable of a limited amount of intellectual activity, and can acquire knowledge within the scope of that activity.[33] Regarding the ability of a moron to elicit a valid matrimonial consent, it may be stated with certainty that some morons can and do validly marry. The mental age of the moron, ranging as it does between eight and twelve years, indicates that a moron can be endowed with the mental capacity to give his consent for marriage. Moreover, a mature moron through the experiences of daily life acquires knowledge which makes him superior to children of the same mental age. Through his intellectual activity and the knowledge that can be drawn from the sensations of puberty it is possible for him to attain to that degree of knowledge that would enable him to elicit a valid consent for marriage.

No definite norm exists for determining just when a moron

[32] S. R. R., *Nullitatis Matrimonii*, 14 nov. 1919, coram R. P. D. Ioanne Prior, dec. XIX, nn. 8-10 — *S. R. R. Decisiones*, XI (1919), 175.

[33] Murray, *Introductory Sociology*, p. 217.

is to be considered capable of giving his consent for marriage.[34] Each case must be considered in the light of its own merits or demerits if one is to determine whether a particular moron has knowledge and discretion which is proportionate to the demand which a contract as serious as that of marriage postulates for him.

In practice, when the validity of a marriage is impugned on the ground of any mental defect, the initial presumption favors the validity of the contract.[35] Sanity and normal development represent the natural state of the mind.[36] It must be proved, therefore, that a mental defect existed and actually vitiated the matrimonial consent, if the granting of a declaration of nullity is to become possible. This proof is provided by witnesses to the marriage and by experts in the field of psychiatry and mental diseases.[37] If both the circumstances surrounding the act of consent and also the testimony given by the experts indicate that a person was laboring under a prohibitive mental defect at the time when the consent was given, then and only then may a marriage be declared invalid.

B. Physical Defects

Thus far consideration has been given to defects in the mind itself which militate against the acquisition of knowledge, and which, therefore, preclude the possibility for the giving of a valid matrimonial consent. An investigation of the process of cognition gives evidence of another group of defects, which in spite of the natural mental capacity of the individual retard or impede the acquisition of knowledge. These defects are found in the physical organs which are the initiators of the mental process.

34 The writer is dealing here with the elements of discretion and knowledge in relation to the nature and essence of marriage. The norma proposed for cases of the insane in which the act of consent is modified and influenced in virtue of past deliberation and formerly possessed knowledge does not apply in this case.

35 Cf. canon 1014.

36 Sanchez, *op. cit.*, lib. I, disp. VIII, n. 17.

37 Cf. canon 1982.

All knowledge, whether sensitive or intellectual, has its genesis in the sensations of qualities produced by an external object stimulating the sense organs.[38] The sense organs are the point of contact between external reality and the mind. The senses operating in their respective organs convey the qualities of an object to the mind, where they are integrated for the forming of a percept or a mental image of the object. The intellect then abstracts the essential notes of the object from the percept to form the abstract concept, the medium of intellectual knowldge.[39] Thus the prime matter of sensitive and intellectual knowledge is supplied by the senses operating in their physical organs.

If the physical organs wherein the senses lie are defective and the senses unable to operate, the prime motor of the cognitive process is lost. As a consequence knowledge cannot be acquired. But knowledge of the essence of marriage is a requisite for the valid contracting of marriage.[40] Therefore, it becomes evident that physical defects which impede the acquisition of knowledge can affect the validity of a marriage contract, inasmuch as the lack of sense perception resulting from such defects gives rise to ignorance which in itself is directly opposed to the possible giving of a matrimonial consent.[41]

In dealing with physical defects and their relationship to matrimonial consent one must recall that the abstract concept of marriage as well as the essential notes of the contract pertain to intellectual knowledge. Therefore, only those defects which render the acquisition of intellectual knowledge impossible or difficult can be said to be opposed to the giving of a valid matrimonial consent. Sight and hearing are pre-eminent in their contribution to intellectual knowledge.[42] They represent the ordinary

38 Dubray, *Introductory Philosophy* (New York, Longmans, Green & Co., 1933), pp. 48, 51.

39 Dubray, *ibidem*, pp. 61, 112; Hickey, *Summula Philosophiae Scholasticae*, II (7. ed., New York, 1927), p. 373; Esser, *Psychologia* (Techny, Ill., 1931), p. 211.

40 Cf. canon 1082, §1.

41 Cf. canon 1082, §1.

42 Hickey, *op. cit.*, II, 296; Esser, *op. cit.*, p. 28.

means of acquiring knowledge of the essence of marriage. Defects in the organs of sight and hearing, then, must be considered in any appraisal of how these defects may exert an effect on the matrimonial consent. This may best be accomplished through the presentation of concrete examples in regard to persons who are deaf, dumb, or blind.

In general, the defects whereby a person is rendered deaf, dumb, or blind constitute hindrances to the contracting of a valid marriage only in so far as they prevent the afflicted person from knowing what marriage is. If the afflictions are sustained after a valid contract has been formed, the marriage bond perdures. Likewise, if a person becomes afflicted in this manner after he has acquired sufficient knowledge for the valid contracting of marriage, the consent thereupon given can exist as a valid matrimonial consent. In both cases the parties enjoy the necessary knowledge for the instituting of a valid contract. Since it is only on the basis of a lack of knowledge that the given defects constitute a hindrance to the giving of consent, both the marriage bond and the consent must be considered valid.

It may be stated also as a general principle that no single defect can adversely affect the validity of a matrimonial consent. If a person is unable to see, the burden of acquiring information through intellectual activity is readily assumed by the sense of hearing. This sense of itself is an adequate channel for the acquisition of knowledge. Conversely, if one's hearing has been destroyed, then the sense of sight may furnish the necessary data. Ideas and thoughts may be conveyed through the use of signs which the sense of sight relays to the mind. It is only a combination of defects that can occasion the lack of a sufficient knowledge, and therefore, only a combination of defects will suffice to affect adversely the validity of a matrimonial consent.[43]

Physical defects in the sense organs of speech, sight and hearing may exist in four different combinations. A person may be: (1) deaf and dumb; (2) deaf, dumb and blind; (3) deaf and blind; or (4) dumb and blind.

43 Sanchez, *De Sancto Matrimonii Sacramento*, lib. I, disp. VIII, nn. 1, 13; Pirhing, *Ius Canonicum*, lib. IV, tit. I, sect. I, n. 2.

(1) Persons who are deaf and dumb (deaf-mutes, as they are called) as a rule elicit a valid matrimonial consent. They can ordinarily acquire the necessary knowledge of the essential notes of marriage through the use of signs.[44] However, if a person is capable only of acquiring sense perceptions of the visible and material things which he sees and touches, but lacks the power of mentally apprehending things in their abstract nature, he cannot give a valid matrimonial consent and validly contract marriage, for in such a case the fundamental concepts of right and obligation which pertain to the essence of marriage are not understood, and as a result the right is not knowingly given or the obligation knowingly undertaken.[45]

(2) When a person is congenitally deaf, dumb and blind, he is, practically considered, incapable of eliciting a valid matrimonial consent. Such a person has no way of knowing what marriage is. He neither can learn through the use of signs nor can he be taught by word of mouth. He must glean his knowledge of the meaning of marriage through the senses of touch and smell, senses which can contribute but little matter for the initiation of rational activity.[46]

A blind deafmute may have derived some knowledge pertinent to marriage through his natural reason and through the promptings arising from the sensations consequent to puberty, but such knowledge takes him scarcely beyond the sense knowledge of brute animals, and does not seem to satisfy the requirements for the issuance of a valid matrimonial consent.[47] However, a valid marriage on the part of a blind deaf-mute is not an absolute

44 C. 23, X, *de sponsalibus et matrimoniis,* IV, I; Sanchez, *loc. cit.;* Pirhing, *loc. cit.*

45 "Si nullam habuisset ideam rerum abstractarum vel intellectualem, non potuisset certe matrimonium contrahere." — *S. R. R. Decisiones,* anno 1764, dec. XX, n. 12.

46 Hostiensis, *Commentaria in Quinque Decretalium Libros,* c. 23, *de spons. et matr.,* IV, I, n. 3; Panormitanus, *Commentaria in Quinque Libros Decretalium,* c. 23, *de spons. et matr.,* IV, I, n. 6; Wex, *Doctrina Theorico-practica SS. Canonum,* pars V, tract. II, c. III, n. 5.

47 Panormitanus, *loc. cit.*

impossibility. The mind of such a person may be perfectly normal. It may for its intellectual operation need no more than the stimulus of impressions derivable through the sense of touch. Given the proper circumstances and opportunities, it is conceivably possible for a blind deaf-mute to acquire a sufficient knowledge for the giving of a valid consent for marriage.[48]

(3) One who is deaf and blind from birth labors under the same difficulty as the blind deaf-mute, for he too is deprived of the ordinary means whereby he may acquire knowledge of the nature of marriage, namely, through signs and by word of mouth.[49]

(4) The condition of the blind mute approximates that of the deaf-mute. Although he is deprived of the sense of sight, he can still be taught the meaning of the marriage contract by word of mouth. Thus he may be considered capable of giving a valid consent based on sufficient knowledge.

In every case of physical affliction affecting the senses of speech, sight, and hearing, primary consideration must be given not to the ability of the afflicted party to acquire knowledge, but rather to the presence or absence of the necessary knowledge when the contract was formed, for a marriage can be contracted validly only when a person actually knows what marriage is, and that he is here and now contracting marriage.[50] If a person in spite of his physical afflictions understands all that pertains to the essence of the marriage contract, he can elicit a valid matrimonial consent and validly contract marriage.

Although the ability of the deaf, dumb, and blind to contract marriage validly may not be denied in the face of a sufficient knowledge, a question may arise, as in the case of the mentally deficient, concerning the licitness of such a marriage. Marriages contracted by persons who are deaf, dumb, and blind are licit or illicit in accordance with the ability or inability of the contracting parties to fulfill the obligations of the marriage state, par-

48 Cappello, *De Matrimonio*, n. 579.

49 Sanchez, *ibidem*, n. 14.

50 Cf. canon 1082, §1.

ticularly with regard to the care and the education of the children. Circumstances of legitimation and solemnization after a civil ceremony may generally be considered as favoring licitness for the contracting of the marriage.

Article II — Incidental Causes of Contingent Ignorance

An incidental cause of contingent ignorance is understood to mean a transient cause of a temporary mental disorder or mental state that is opposed to the execution of a deliberate act. It is called an incidental cause in contradistinction to the aforementioned subsistent cause, which produces a permanent state of ignorance. Contingent ignorance resulting from an incidental cause pertains to a case in which a party to a marriage has a habitual knowledge of the essence of marriage, but cannot or does not apply his knowledge or exercise the proper amount of deliberation in the act of marrying.

The simplest example of an incidental cause of contingent ignorance is over-indulgence in the use of intoxicating drinks, or drunkenness, as the resultant condition is called. Excessive use of intoxicating drinks has a destructive effect on mental activity. It takes away the use of reason and consequently renders the intoxicated person incapable of performing any human act. Thus a person may have habitually a sufficient knowledge of the marriage contract to enable him to give a valid consent for marriage, but because of his state of inebriation may not at the time of the formation of the contract have the requisite mental capacity to apply the habitually possessed knowledge regarding marriage to the act whereby the marriage contract is formed. In other words, an intoxicated person may know habitually what marriage is, but may not realize that he is here and now contracting marriage.

Drunkenness by its very nature admits of varying degrees. This divergence depends not only on the quantity of intoxicants consumed, but also on the manner in which they affect a given person under specific physical circumstances. The mental capacity of the inebriated person exists in inverse proportion to the state of inebriation. The more inebriated a person becomes, the more he is deprived of the faculty of deliberation.

Since drunkenness and its consequent mental incapacity admit of degrees, it is necessary to determine what stages of intoxication hinder the eliciting of a valid matrimonial consent. Certainly a slight exhilaration caused by intoxicating drink does not imply a vitiation of the matrimonial consent. The faculty of reason is not so impaired that deliberation is impossible. It is equally certain that the state of complete inebriation, in which the inebriate is wholly deprived of the use of reason, makes it impossible for him to elicit a valid consent for marriage.[51] To determine the degree of intoxication that hinders the giving of a valid matrimonial consent, one may employ the norm used in cases of progressive and stabilized semi-insanity; if a person, while under the influence of intoxicating drink, is capable of that degree of deliberation which is postulated for the committing of a mortal sin, he is capable also of furnishing a valid consent for marriage.

It is presupposed that the inebriated person has a habitual knowledge of the essence of marriage and of the seriousness of the contract. In the act of marrying he must apply his knowledge regarding the essence of marriage in order that his act of consent may be a deliberate act. In accordance with the degree of application of which he is capable, his consent is to be regarded as valid or as invalid. The application of knowledge in the performance of an act, or deliberation, as it is called, determines the degree of a person's responsibility for the act he performs. If a person employs that degree of deliberation which in the commission of a gravely sinful act makes him responsible for a mortal sin, he elicits a valid matrimonial consent and enters a valid matrimonial union.

In applying the norm one must be careful to distinguish between the voluntary consent given merely in conformity with the required marriage form[52] and the voluntary consent given with an understanding of the nature and impart of the marriage con-

51 Boich, *Commentaria in Quinque Decretalium Libros*, c. 24, *de spons. et matr.*, IV, I, n. 4; Leurenius, *Ius Canonicum Universum*, lib. IV, tit. I, q. 100; Gasparri, *Tractatus Canonicus de Matrimonio*, II, n. 886; Vlaming, *Praelectiones Iuris Matrimonii*, II, n. 521.

52 Cf. canon 1094.

tract. A distinction also must be made in the case of the former between one who has a habitual will to marry and one who has only a conceptual knowledge of marriage. A person may have a habitual will to contract marriage, and at the time of the marriage ceremony, though inebriated, he may be capable of the voluntary act whereby he expresses his will to marry without, however, having at that time the necessary appreciation of what the marriage contract involves. The marriage must be held to be valid in this case in consequence of the previous will to contract marriage, even though the inebriated person is at the time capable of that deliberation which is postulated for the commission of a mortal sin. The application of the norm is reserved rather to a case in which a person has had no more than a conceptual knowledge of marriage without ever having arrived at an appreciation of marriage as directed to his own person.

Thus an inebriated person may be capable of executing all the formalities connected with the marriage ceremony, and may also have a notion of what marriage is and that he is contracting marriage, but he may at the same time fail to appreciate the seriousness of what he is doing. Such a person cannot be said to consent to marriage or to contract it validly, for a mere conceptual knowledge without a practical appreciation *(cognitio aestimativa)* of marriage does not constitute a sufficient knowledge for the formation of a marriage contract.[53] It is in contemplation of such a case that the norm is proposed, namely, that a person who is capable of that degree of deliberation which is postulated for the commission of mortal sin is to be considered as having the mental capacity to evaluate the nature and impart of marriage.

Narcotics are equivalent to intoxicating drinks in their effect on matrimonial consent. They impair the activity of the intellect and interfere with the process of deliberation. The effect of narcotics on matrimonial consent, like the effect of intoxicating drinks, is measured by the amount taken and the resultant effect

53 Anonymous, "De Cognitione Aestimativa in Matrimonio" — *Periodica de Re Morali, Canonica, Liturgica,* XXX (1941), 6-12.

upon a given person under specific physical circumstances. If the drugs administered bring about a state of unconsciousness or the complete loss of the use of reason, no deliberation is possible, and consequently a valid matrimonial consent cannot be given. If the use of reason is not lost but only impaired, then the degree of deliberation of which a person is capable determines the validity or the invalidity of the consent, and the degree of deliberation which suffices for the commission of a mortal sin is to be acknowledged as sufficing also for the giving of a valid matrimonial consent and the contracting of a valid marriage.

Delirium, too, is an incidental cause of contingent ignorance. Delirium represents a temporary state of mental incapacity arising from a physical illness. It is usually associated with fever. A delirious person because of his mental incapacity is deprived of the faculty of deliberation, and therefore cannot elicit a valid matrimonial consent.[54]

The category further includes hypnosis, somnambulism, and even inadvertence. A hypnotized person and a somnambulist are capable of unconscious activity only. They have no deliberate contact with external reality. The acts they perform cannot be called deliberate acts. In view of their indeliberate and unconscious activity they cannot be said to know what they are doing, and accordingly cannot validly give consent for marriage.

Inadvertence, considered as a cause of contingent ignorance, contemplates a case in which a person, endowed not only with a sufficient knowledge but also with a sound mind, does not advert to the fact that he is contracting marriage in consequence of some intense concentration on or preoccupation with some other object. A consent thus given is equivalent to a simulated consent, inasmuch as there is no conformity between the external act and the internal intention. He does not know and realize that he is here and now entering into a contract. Consequently his consent is neither deliberate nor true, and accordingly no valid marriage is effected.

54 S. R. R., *Nullitatis Matrimonii,* 23 mart. 1914, coram R. P. D. Guilelmo Sebastianelli, dec. XII — *S. R. R. Decisiones,* VI (1914), 144-145.

Article III — Marriage Effected by Virtual Consent

Inasmuch as the consent of the parties is the efficient cause of the marriage contract,[55] defective mental states vitiate the contract only when the resultant ignorance is coincident with the time when the consent is given. However, the consent of the contracting parties, although it must be a mutual consent,[56] need not be more than morally simultaneous,[57] that is, the consent of both parties need not be given at exactly the same time.[58] It suffices that the consent of one party still continue when the other party elicits his or her consent, so that at some particular moment there is a deliberate union of wills relative to the formation of a marriage contract.[59] The question, therefore, arises whether a mentally defective person can enter into a valid marriage by virtue of a consent given at some previous time when he was of sound mind, in possession of the necessary knowledge, and capable of sufficient deliberation to elicit a valid matrimonial consent.

Consent may be considered as having been elicited simply as prior to the consent of the other party, or as prior to the renewed consent of the other party, when that renewal is required for the convalidation of a marriage which was invalid by reason of some previously existing diriment impediment. A consent elicited before the celebration of the marriage, and consequently before the consent of the other party, cannot form the basis for a valid marriage contract when the party who issued the previous consent suffers a mental lapse before the actual celebration of the

55 Cf. canon 1081, §1.

56 Cf. canon 1081, §2.

57 Sanchez, *op. cit.*, lib. IV, disp. XXVIII, n. 1; Schmalzgrueber, *Ius Ecclesiasticum Universum*, lib. IV, tit. I, n. 261; Cappello, *De Matrimonio*, n. 576.

58 The efficacy of virtual consent in contracting marriage is acknowledged and exemplified by the code in dealing with cases of simple convalidation and radical sanation. — Cf. canons 1133; 1135, §3; 1136; 1138, §1-3; 1139, §1.

59 De Becker, *De Sponsalibus et Matrimonio Praelectiones Canonicae* (2. ed., Lovanii, New York, 1903), p. 27.

marriage.[60] It is true of course that a virtual consent suffices for the contracting of a valid marriage,[61] but a person who has lost the use of his reason does not furnish a virtual consent for marriage in view simply of the previous act of his will.[62] The defective mental state completely destroys the force of the previous consent, so that there is no union of wills from which a marriage bond could arise.[63] As a result the consent of the parties is neither physically nor morally simultaneous, and therefore lacks the character of reciprocity which is necessary for a valid marriage contract.[64]

For the simple convalidation of a marriage which was invalid in consequence of a previously existing diriment impediment, the Code demands that the consent be renewed by at least one of the contracting parties.[65] Would the renewal of consent by one of the parties suffice to constitute a valid marriage if the other party to the contract, who at the time of the marriage ceremony gave a true matrimonial consent, has become deprived of the use of reason? If the loss of the use of reason is attributable to insanity, the marriage cannot be convalidated. The efficacy of the unilateral renewal of consent depends upon the perseverance of the consent of the other party.[66] Since the will for the contract of marriage has ceased to exist in an insane person,[67] it cannot be said that his will perseveres. Consequently there is no furnishing of mutual consent on the side of both of the parties, and hence also no convalidation of the marriage.

However, if the mental state is affected by an incidental cause, such as drunkenness or somnambulism, the renewal of

60 Sanchez, *De Sancto Matrimonii Sacramento*, lib. I, disp. VIII, n. 20.

61 Gasparri, *Tractatus Canonicus de Matrimonio*, II, n. 879.

62 De Lugo, *Disputationes Scholasticae et Morales* (8 vols., Parisiis, 1869), III, *Tractatus de Sacramentis in Genere*, disp. VIII, n. 108; Wernz, *Ius Decretalium* (2. ed., 6 vols., Romae et Prati, 1906-1913), IV, n. 45, ad annot. (94).

63 Gasparri, *ibidem*, n. 973.

64 Cf. canon 1081, §2.

65 Cf. canon 1133, §1.

66 Cf. canons 1135, §3; 1136, §1.

67 De Lugo, *loc. cit.*

consent by one party suffices to effect a valid marriage, for in this instance the use of reason is not destroyed in the other party, but merely suspended, and the consent of the mentally defective party continues to exist, and accordingly combines with the expressly renewed consent of the other party to constitute a truly mutual consent for the marriage.[68]

A peculiar situation arises when a marriage becomes radically sanated. A radical sanation implies a dispensation from the law that calls for a renewal of the consent.[69] Can the concession of a radical sanation by competent ecclesiastical authority effect the validity of a marriage which previously existed as an invalid union in the face of some ecclesiastical impediment, when one of the parties who gave a true matrimonial consent at the time of the marriage ceremony has since lapsed into a mental state which is opposed to the execution of a valid matrimonial consent? The problem and its solution are similar to those proposed in the case of simple convalidation. The efficacy of a radical sanation is dependent upon the perseverance of the consent of both parties to the contract.[70] If a person becomes insane, the use of reason is destroyed and with it the efficacious continuance of the previous consent.[71] Since there is lacking even a virtual consent, the radical sanation cannot effect a validation, for the lack of consent inherently connotes the absence of a condition essential to the contract, and as such is beyond remedy by means of a radical sanation.[72]

If a party to a marriage suffers a temporary loss of the use of reason as the result of an incidental cause, the radical sanation secures its effect and the marriage becomes validated, for in such a case, since the use of reason is merely suspended,[73] a virtual consent is present, and thus a mutual consent for marriage is furnished by the two parties.

68 Gasparri, *loc. cit.*
69 Cf. canon 1138, §1.
70 Cf. canon 1139, §1.
71 De Lugo, *loc. cit.;* Wernz, *loc. cit.;* Gasparri, *loc. cit.*
72 Cf. canon 1139, §2.
73 Gasparri, *op. cit.*, II, n. 973.

ARTICLE IV — MARRIAGE BY PROXY

According to law the will of the parties to contract a marriage may be indicated by the parties themselves or through the instrumentality of a proxy.[74] The proxy in a marriage receives a mandate authorizing him to contract marriage in the name of his principal.[75] The competence of the proxy in the execution of the mandate is measured by that of the party whom he represents, so that he can do or intend no more than the party himself would to or intend were he to act personally. Consequently, if the party to the contract lapses into insanity after he has given his mandate, but before it has been executed by the proxy, the consent conveyed by the proxy does not effect a valid matrimonial contract.[76] The consent of the insane principal has ceased to exist, and the mandate has lost all its force.[77]

When the proxy acts, after the principal has lapsed into insanity, he no longer performs a deliberate act in the name of his principal. This remains true whether the state of insanity is permanent or merely temporary.[78] If the person who issued a mandate to a proxy became insane, but thereupon before the celebration of the marriage ceremony again regained his sanity, he would need to issue a new mandate to the proxy, for the original mandate carried with it a consent that ceased to exist when the principal became insane.

A valid marriage may be contracted in virtue of a mandate given to a proxy if the mental defect of the principal is but a temporary defect produced by an incidental cause; then the use of reason is merely suspended, and the consent of the principal virtually persists and therefore combines with the expressed consent of the other party to effect a mutual valid consent for the matrimonial contract.[79]

74 Cf. canon 1089, §1.

75 Cf. canon 1089, §1.

76 Cf. canon 1089, §3.

77 De Lugo, *Disputationes Scholasticae et Morales*, III, *Tractatus de Sacramentis in Genere*, disp. VIII, n. 108.

78 Cappello, *De Matrimonio*, n. 619.

79 Gasparri, *Tractatus Canonicus de Matrimonio*, II, 973.

CHAPTER V

SUBSISTENT IGNORANCE

The term "subsistent ignorance" is used to designate the lack of knowledge that attaches to a normal and sound mind. It may be identified with a lack of sufficient maturity of judgment in evaluating and understanding the complex concept of marriage, or simply with a lack of intellectual activity relative to the contract of marriage, inasmuch as the marriage contract with all its essential characteristics was never introduced into the intellect as an object of cognition, in which case a person is said to be ignorant of the nature of the marriage contract for the simple reason that he has never given it any or sufficient thought. In view of this twofold causality of subsistent ignorance, a matrimonial consent is said to be rendered invalid on the ground of a lack of sufficient discretion, or simply through the lack of knowledge.

Article I — Lack of Discretion

The validity of a matrimonial consent is dependent upon the discretion of the contracting parties, inasmuch as they must be so intellectually mature as to be able to understand the nature and import of the marriage contract, and the rights and obligations that it entails.[1] When the intellectual faculty has not been developed to this degree of perfection, then the parties cannot be said to give a valid matrimonial consent or to enter a valid matrimonial union.

A. *The Age of Discretion*

The intellectual faculty develops with the increasing age of the individual. Therefore it is of practical import to consider the mental capacity of persons individually and their consequent ability or inability to contract marriage on the basis of the age in years that they have attained.

[1] Gasparri, *Tractatus Canonicus de Matrimonio,* II, n. 881; Cappello, *De Matrimonio,* n. 581.

A person who has not reached the age of seven is presumed by law to be *non sui compos*.[2] Such a person is presumed not to have acquired the use of reason. Since presumably he is not capable of making a judgment mature or otherwise, he presumably also lacks a sufficient discretion for the eliciting of a valid matrimonial consent. Thus Gratian declared that persons who gave their children in marriage accomplished nothing unless the children themselves upon reaching the age of discretion consented to the union.[3]

Similarly, one who has reached the age of reason, but who is still at an age proximate to infancy, does not have a sufficient discretion for entering into a contract that is binding either in civil or natural law.[4] The possession and the use of reason cannot in themselves be used as a criterion for determining the intellectual fitness of a person to contract marriage; for although the age of reason and the age of discretion are said to coincide when consideration is given to the obligation of receiving Communion during the Paschal season,[5] the same is not true when the formation of a marriage contract is under discussion. Over and above the use of reason there is required a maturity of judgment and a measure of discretion proportionate in gravity to that of the marriage contract itself, so that the contracting parties know and understand what pertains to the essence of marriage.[6]

The age of discretion relative to marriage is rather presumed to be coincident with the age of puberty;[7] that is, when a person has reached the age of puberty he is presumed to be

2 Cf. canon 88, §3.

3 C. un., C. XXX, q. 2.

4 Sanchez, *De Sancto Matrimonii Sacramento*, lib. IV, disp. XXXVIII, n. 24; Gasparri, *loc. cit.*

5 Cf. canon 859, §1.

6 St. Thomas, *In 4 Libros Sententiarum*, Lib. IV, dist. 27, q. 2, art. 2, ad 2um — *Opera Omnia*, studio ac labore Stanislai Frette et Pauli Mare (34 vols., Parisiis: Apud L. Vives, 1871-1880); *S. R. R.*, *Nullitatis Matrimonii*, 28 aug. 1911, coram R. P. D. Aloysio Sincero, dec. XXXIX, n. 42 — *S. R. R. Decisiones*, III (1911), 450.

7 Rufinus, *Summa Decretorum*, c. un., C. XXX, q. 2.

endowed with the requisite physical and intellectual qualification for instituting a valid marriage contract.

B. *The Relation between the Age of Puberty and the Age of Discretion*

The age of puberty may be considered in a legal or in a physiological sense.[8] Taken in a legal sense the age of puberty, namely, fourteen years for boys and twelve years for girls,[9] admits of no absolute relationship to the age of discretion. The completion of the fourteenth year does not necessarily imply the existence of a sufficient discretion for the eliciting of a valid matrimonial consent, nor can it be said that one who has not reached the legal age of puberty absolutely lacks a sufficient discretion for the contracting of marriage. The ages of fourteen and twelve years merely represents the time when a boy and girl are presumed to be mentally capable of contracting a valid marriage.[10]

The presumption gives way to contrary proof. The Sacred Congregation of the Council granted a declaration of nullity when it was proved that a girl of nearly thirteen years did not have sufficient knowledge of the essence of marriage.[11] On the other hand, pre-Code law recognized the validity of a marriage contracted before the legal age of puberty when the precocity of the parties supplied for the defect in the lack of age.[12] Thus canonists admitted that a person could have sufficient discretion for the contracting of a valid marriage even before he or she had reached the fourteenth or twelfth year of age.

The physiological age of puberty, that is, the age when the condition of puberty is actually present, is not necessarily indica-

[8] Lanza, *Theologia Moralis Specialis de Matrimonio* (Romae, 1940), p. 457.

[9] Cf. canon 88, §2.

[10] C. 8, X, *de desponsatione impuberum,* IV, 2; Jaffe, n. 13765.

[11] S. C. C., *in Ventimillien.,* 19 maii 1888 — *Thesaurus,* CXVII (1888), 289, 518.

[12] C. 9, X, *de desponsatione impuberum,* IV, 2; Pirhing, *Ius Canonicum,* lib. IV, tit. I, sect. 1, n. 85; Sanchez, *op. cit.,* lib. VII, disp. CIV, n. 5.

tive of the existence of a sufficient discretion for the giving of a valid matrimonial consent. At most it can be stated that ignorance is not presumed after a person has attained to puberty,[13] so that if the validity of a marriage contracted after puberty is impugned on the ground of insufficient knowledge, proof of the existing ignorance must be produced.

The question now arises whether a person can be said to be endowed with a sufficient discretion for the contracting of marriage before he has attained to puberty; in other words, is there an essential relationship of dependence between the state of puberty and the possession of discretion, in the sense that puberty must make an essential contribution to the knowledge content that constitutes the discretion of the contracting parties. Sanchez denied the existence of such an essential relationship. He maintained that a person who was proximate to the state of puberty was usually endowed with a sufficient discretion for the contracting of a valid marriage.[14]

The Sacred Congregation of the Holy Office implied the same thing in a response given to the Vicar Apostolic of Hunan, China. The prelate asked the Holy Office whether infidel children who were married in accordance with the Chinese custom could cohabit, if they were converted with their whole family. The response was to the effect that Christian *impuberes*, if they had contracted marriage while still pagans, had to be separated, but that they would have the obligation of living together matrimonially upon attaining the age of puberty, provided that the marriage was not proved null for lack of consent.[15]

The same Congregation, in response to the question whether spouses who were married while they were pagans before attaining puberty, and who had not consummated their union could be considered as having contracted a true marriage, declared that, as long as it was clear that there was no impediment of the natural or positive divine law, a true marriage contract was

13 Cf. canon 1082, §2.

14 Sanchez, *op. cit.*, lib. VII, disp. CIV, n. 27.

15 S. C. S. Off. (Hunan), 2 maii 1866, ad 2 — *Collectanea S. Congregationis de Propaganda Fide* (2 vols., Romae, 1907), n. 1289.

formed.[16] Since the contract in each of the foregoing cases was made while the parties were still *impuberes,* it was evidently the mind of the Sacred Congregation that a sufficient discretion for the eliciting of a valid matrimonial consent could be had before the attainment of puberty

Gasparri explicitly states that there can be no doubt that a true matrimonial consent can be given before the attainment of puberty.[17] He is followed in this opion by all modern authors who argue that the status of puberty is required only in consequence of ecclesiastical law, and consequently a marriage contracted according to the natural law is valid if the contracting parties know what marriage is, even though they have not attained to the physical condition of puberty.[18]

Puberty, therefore, can at most give rise to a presumption for or against ignorance, insofar as ignorance can be presumed before puberty, or cannot be presumed after puberty.[19] There is no definite essential relationship between puberty and discretion. Puberty is associated with discretion only for the reason that puberty is reached at an age when the intellectual faculty is believed to have had sufficient time to develop to a point at which discretion may be presumed as present.

The lack of discretion as a hindrance to marriage had more extensive application in the pre-Code law. When the Code raised the requisite age for a valid marriage to sixteen years for boys and fourteen years for girls,[20] it eliminated to a great extent the possibility of the contracting of a marriage in the face of such an existing hindrance. However, the question of the presence of the necessary discretion is of practical importance with reference to marriages contracted by infidels, who are not bound by the ecclesiastical impediment of nonage,[21] but who are bound

16 S. C. S. Off., 10 dec. 1885 — *Fontes,* n. 1097.

17 Gasparri, *op. cit.,* I, n. 546.

18 Vlaming, *Praelectiones Iuris Matrimonii,* I, n. 260; Wernz-Vidal, *Ius Matrimoniale,* n. 207; Chelodi, *Ius Matrimoniale,* n. 68; Gougnard, *Tractatus de Matrimonio,* n. 375.

19 Gasparri, *op. cit.,* II, 882.

20 Cf. canon 1067, §1.

21 Cf. canon 87.

only by the natural law which demands the presence of the necessary discretion for the instituting of a valid marriage.

Article II — Lack of Knowledge

The validity of a matrimonial consent demands, aside from the intellectual maturity which implies an understanding of the meaning of the matrimonial rights and obligations, and of the import of the matrimonial contract binding for the future, that specific knowledge which is peculiar to the marriage contract, that is, that knowledge which makes the agreement of the parties a marital agreement, and distinguishes the matrimonial contract from any other type of contract. Therefore, in order that a person may be said to be endowed with the requisite mental capacity for eliciting a valid matrimonial consent, he must be capable of making a judgment concerning the nature and the import of a contract that has as its object the permanent union of a man and a woman for the procreation of children.

Specific knowledge of the nature of the marriage contract is not the necessary complement of intellectual maturity. A person may have developed his intellectual faculty to such a degree of perfection that he has no difficulty in understanding the general nature of a contract and the notions of right and obligation, but at the same time he may know nothing of marriage as a contract, or he may be ignorant of an essential element of the marriage contract. However, in view of the social nature of man and the common evidence of family society a person is not presumed to be lacking in the knowledge necessary for eliciting a valid matrimonial consent after he has reached the age of puberty.[22]

The age of puberty, which is indicative of the time after which a person is not presumed to be ignorant of the essential elements of marriage, is understood to mean the legal or juridic age of puberty,[23] namely, fourteen and twelve years, the ages

22 Cf. canon 1082, §2.

23 Fourneret, *Le Mariage Chrétien* (Paris, 1919), p. 115; Manning, *Presumption of Law in Matrimonial Procedure,* The Catholic University of America Canon Law Studies, n. 94 (Washington, D. C.: The Catholic University of America, 1935), p. 74.

when a boy and girl respectively are presumed by law to be *puberes*.[24] Accordingly, a boy who has completed his fourteenth year, or a girl who has completed her twelfth year, is not presumed to be ignorant of the import of marriage. On the other hand, a boy and girl who have not reached these respective ages are presumed to be laboring under such ignorance, and must prove that they have the necessary knowledge before they can be permitted to marry.[25]

In practice, when the validity of a contracted marriage is impugned on the ground of ignorance, the existence of such ignorance must be conclusively proved. This is true whether the marriage in question was contracted by persons bound by ecclesiastical law, or by those who are subject exclusively to the natural law. Persons who are bound by ecclesiastical law cannot validly marry until they are two years beyond the juridic age of puberty.[26] Consequently, when they contract marriage in accordance with the law they are not presumed to be ignorant. If marriage is contracted with a dispensation from the ecclesiastical impediment of nonage, proof of the ignorance must be produced either in virtue 1082, § 2, when marriage is contracted after the juridic age of puberty, or in virtue of canon 1014—which states that a presumption of law favors the validity of a contracted marriage—when marriage is contracted before that age.

Those who are not bound by ecclesiastical law must likewise prove the existence of invalidating ignorance; for marriage once contracted remains in possession until the existence of some hindrance which vitiated the contract is proved. The provision of canon 1014 regarding the presumption in favor of the validity of marriage is to be applied to every marriage, whether it is contracted between Catholics, between non-Catholics, or between infidels.[27]

24 Cf. canon 88, §2.

25 Gasparri, *op. cit.*, II, n. 882; Cappello, *De Matrimonio*, n. 582.

26 Cf. canons 88, §2; 1067, §1.

27 *Collectanea S. C. Congregationis de Propaganda Fide*, n. 1392; Vermeersch-Creusen, *Epitome Iuris Canonici*, II (5. ed., Bruxellis, 1934), n. 279; Cappello, *De Matrimonio*, n. 53.

CHAPTER VI

THE EXTENT OF INVALIDATING IGNORANCE

Although the consent of the parties to a marriage contract must be a deliberate consent, it would be wrong to suppose that ignorance of anything without limitation pertaining to marriage could vitiate a matrimonial consent and thereby affect the validity of a marriage contract.[1] It is necessary but also sufficient for the validity of any contract that the contracting parties know what pertains to the essence of the contract. Since marriage partakes of the nature of a true bilateral contract,[2] only that ignorance can be said to affect the validity of a matrimonial consent, and consequently the validity of a marriage, which is directly related to those elements which are essential to marriage. It was noted in the consideration of the general notions of marriage that marriage admits of an essential object, essential ends and essential properties; therefore, for the validity of a matrimonial consent it is indeed necessary, but it is also sufficient, that the contracting parties be not ignorant of the essential object, ends, and properties of marriage, or specifically that they be not ignorant of the fact that marriage is a permanent society between a man and a woman for the procreation of children.[3]

Article I — Ignorance of the Object of Marriage

Canon 1082, § 1, provides that the parties to a marriage contract must know that marriage is a society.[4] To know that marriage is a society is to know that marriage involves rights and obligations, and that the end of marriage is to be attained by the corporate activity of the parties; for a society is essen-

1 Pallottini, *s. v. Matrimonium,* III, *Quoad Consensum,* n. 6.

2 Cappello, *De Matrimonio,* n. 23.

3 Cf. canon 1082, §1.

4 "Ut matrimonialis consensus haberi possit, necesse est ut contrahentes saltem non ignorant matrimonium esse societatem permanentem inter virum et mulierem ad filios procreandos."

tially a moral union of intelligent beings, bound by rights and obligations, and co-operating together to effect a common end.[5]

Canon 1082, § 1, therefore, at least implies that a person who marries must know that in a marital union he is under an obligation to do what is necessary in order that the end of marriage may be attained. Without some realization of the existence of a right and a corresponding obligation on the part of the spouses the union lacks stability, or even existence. It is not a union as evidenced in the concept of society, namely a union founded upon a real and permanent bond; it is rather a precarious union governed by the actual will of the parties. If a person marries without realizing that he is conceding a right, without knowing that he is binding himself, that he owes something to his partner in marriage, he is but giving his consent to the performance of one or more acts whereby children are begotten, and not to the concession and acceptance of a corporal right which is the essential object of the matrimonial consent.[6] Such a person is consenting to corporate activity rather than to the formation of a conjugal society, and as a result every exercise of the conjugal act in its nature of a right and duty depends on a new act of the will.

The obligation and the right from which the obligation flows must be specified by the intellect, that is, the parties to the marriage contract must know and will the concession and acceptance of the particular right and obligation peculiar to marriage.[7] The rights and obligations proper to any society are determined by the end for which the society was created.[8] Since the end of the conjugal society is the procreation of offspring, those who enter into a conjugal union must know and will to concede and accept the rights and obligations whereby the end of the conjugal

5 Hickey, *Summula Philosophiae Scholasticae*, III (7 ed., Herder, 1934), n. 470; Vermeersch, *Principia-Responsa-Consilia, Theologiae Moralis*, II, n. 453.

6 Cf. canon 1081, §2.

7 Wernz-Vidal, *Ius Matrimoniale*, n. 457; Vlaming, *Praelectiones Iuris Matrimonii*, II, n. 524; Gougnard, *Tractatus de Matrimonio*, p. 150.

8 Hickey, *loc. cit.*

society, the procreation of offspring, may be realized;[9] or, more specifically, they must know and will to concede and accept the right to each other's body for the performance of those acts which of themselves are ordained for the procreation of offspring.[10]

This conclusion is demanded by both the nature of society in general and the nature of the conjugal society in particular, and by the notion of matrimonial consent, which is precisely defined as being an act of the will by which both parties to a marriage give and accept the perpetual and exclusive right to each other's body for the performance of those acts which serve the effect of generation.[11] The concession and acceptances of the corporal right is the essential object of the matrimonial consent.[12] In contracting marriage a person wills to concede and accept the corporal right, and therefore he must have knowledge of such a right by reason of the general principle that nothing can be willed unless it is first known.

The concession and acceptance of the corporal right need not be explicitly willed or intended by the parties to a marriage contract. It suffices for the validity of a marriage contract that the contracting parties explicitly will or intend to do what others do when they marry, or to contract marriage as it was instituted by God, and thus only implicitly to will that all that pertains to the essence of marriage.[13] However, the sufficiency of such a general intention does not eliminate the necessity for knowledge of the corporal right, nor is the implicit intention of the parties to be taken as a substitute for knowledge of the essential elements of marriage.[14]

9 Augustine, *A Commentary on the New Code of Canon Law* (8 vols., St. Louis: Herder & Co., 1918-1921), Vol. V (revised edition, 1920), p. 227.

10 Ayrinhac-Lydon, *Marriage Legislation in the New Code of Canon Law* (revised edition, New York: Benziger Brothers, 1940), p. 193.

11 S. R. R., *Nullitatis Matrimonii*, 2 aug. 1929, coram R. P. D. Maximo Massimi, Decano, dec. XLIII, n. 2 — *S. R. R. Decisiones*, XXI (1929), 365.

12 Ayrinhac-Lydon, *loc. cit.*

13 Gasparri, *Tractatus Canonicus de Matrimonio*, II, n. 901.

14 Woywod, *A Practical Commentary on the Code of Canon Law* (5. ed., 2 vols., New York, 1939), I, 650.

The will to contract marriage must be founded on the knowledge of what marriage is in its essence according to the provision of canon 1082, § 1. The essential elements of marriage, whether they are willed explicitly or implicitly, must be known by the contracting parties. If a person in marrying has the general will to do what others do when they marry, his consent is valid only insofar as his understanding of what others do in marrying comprehends all that is essential to the marriage contract. Thus, if a person were to think that marriage consisted merely of cohabitation and companionship, though he likewise had the general intention to do what others do when they marry, he would not validly contract marriage, for his general intention is governed by the knowledge regarding marriage that he actually possesses. With such limited knowledge he is consenting but to cohabitation and companionship, and not to the concession and acceptance of a permanent and exclusive corporal right, which has as its object the performance of those acts which are ordained for the procreation of children.

In practice, when a person consents to contract marriage as it is contracted by others he is said to will implicitly all that pertains to marriage in view of the fact that ignorance is not presumed to affect the consent of a person who has reached the age of puberty. It does not necessarily follow, therefore, that a person who contracts marriage with such a general consent actually has the requisite knowledge.

Admitting the necessity for knowledge concerning the concession and acceptance of the corporal right for the performance of acts ordained for the procreation of offspring, one may ask whether the validity of a matrimonial consent requires the specification of those acts which are the object of the corporal right; that is, whether persons who give their consent for marriage must have knowledge of the conjugal act or of carnal copulation.

Gasparri declares that, if a girl in marrying knows that marriage is a union with a man who together with a woman procreates children that are born of the woman, she has a sufficient knowledge to elicit a valid matrimonial consent, even though she does not know that children are begotten through carnal copulation, and likewise has no knowledge whatever of carnal copulation. A girl in consenting to a union for the procreation of children, says Gasparri, implicitly consents to concede the right of coition.[15]

Vlaming (+ 1935) takes exception to the opinion of Gasparri by stating that the concept of carnal copulation is essentially related to the ideas of conceding the marital right. He believes that the marriage contract is not sufficiently distinguished from other contracts by a person who when marrying does not know that children are had through carnal copulation. Vlaming bases his argument for the necessity of this knowledge on the fact that the right that is given in marriage consists essentially in the power of demanding the use of the body for the procreation of children, and not in the power of procreating children. He does not see how a person can validly concede such a power without knowledge of its object, namely the use of the body or *copula*.[16]

The knowledge of the *copula*, according to Vlaming, need not be physiologically exact, but the parties to a marriage contract must know at least that in order that children may be born of a woman there is required some kind of corporal union.[17]

Knecht (†1932) follows the reasoning of Vlaming.[18] Gougnard and Capello in like vein demand that the parties to a marriage contract know that the procreation of offspring is effected through carnal copulation. Gougnard avers that if a person is ignorant of the manner in which carnal copulation

15 "Si puella nubens scit, e.g., matrimonium esse societatem cum viro, qui ex uxore filios procreat, et in hanc societatem ad filios procreandos consentit, sed nescit filios haberi per carnalem copulam, imo hanc carnalem copulam prorsus ignorat, est casus ignorantiae, quae non excludit matrimonialem consensum et coniugii valorem, cum puella, consentiens in societatem ad filiorum procreationem, implicite consenserit in ipsum coeundi ius." — Gasparri, *op. cit.*, II, n. 901.

16 Vlaming, *Praelectiones Iuris Matrimonii,* II, n. 524.

17 ". . . nostra sententia non postulari scientiam copulae physiologice exactam, sed eam qua nupturiens saltem sciat, ad filios ex uxore procreandos, necessarium esse concursum proprii corporis . . ." — Vlaming, *loc. cit.*

18 Knecht, *Handbuch des katholischen Eherechts* (Freiburg im Breisgau; Herder, 1928), p. 548.

takes place, the matrimonial consent is valid. However, if a person knows that marriage is a society instituted for the procreation of offspring, but does not know that procreation is effected by a carnal union, the consent is invalid for lack of necessary knowledge.[19]

Capello in turn concedes that ignorance of the manner in which children are begotten does not affect the validity of the matrimonial consent. But, he declares, a person who marries must know that procreation takes place as the result of carnal union. Capello requires at least a vague and confused knowledge of carnal union, a carnal union that is proper to marriage alone, so that marriage is distinguished from other contracts; otherwise, he states, there is lacking the proper and specific object of the matrimonial consent.[20]

Oesterle goes further and insists that persons who contract marriage must have a specific knowledge of the carnal act.[21] Wernz-Vidal, Vermeersch-Creusen, Payen, and Chelodi are content, however, to state simply that the contracting parties must know that the procreation of children is effected by a corporal union.[22]

It has been the constant teaching of the Church that the consent of the parties alone is the efficient cause of the marriage contract.[23] The marriage contract, therefore, is perfected by the mutual concession and acceptance of a corporal right for the performance of acts ordained for the procreation of children. The exercise of the corporal right, or the conjugal act, is not in

19 Gougnard, *Tractatus de Matrimonio,* p. 150.

20 Cappello, *op. cit.,* Vol. III, pars II, n. 582.

21 Oesterle, "Nullitas Matrimonii ex Capite Ignorantiae" — *Ephemerides Theologicae Lovanienses* (Lovanii, Universitas Catholica Lovaniensis, 1924—), XV (1938), 547 sq.

22 Wernz-Vidal, *Ius Matrimoniale,* n. 457; Vermeersch-Creusen, *Epitome Iuris Canonici,* II, n. 369; Payen, *De Matrimonio in Missionibus ac Potissimum in Sinis Tractatus Practicus et Casus,* III, nn. 1623-1626; Chelodi, *Ius Matrimoniale,* n. 110.

23 Pope Nicholas I (858-867), c. 2, C. XXVII, q. 2; Pope Innocent III (1198-1216), c. 23, X, *de sponsalibus et matrimoniis,* IV, 1; Pope Eugene IV (1431-1447), const. *"Exultate Deo,"* 22 nov. 1439 — *Bullarium,* V, 51; Pope Urban VIII (1623-1644), const. *"Magnum in Christo," op. cit.,* XIV, 595.

itself necessary for the institution of a valid marriage contract; consequently the conjugal act or carnal copulation does not pertain to the essence of the contract, but is rather an effect thereof.[24]

Since carnal copulation does not pertain to the essence of the marriage contract, ignorance of carnal copulation does not affect the validity of the matrimonial consent. Indeed, whenever a person sought a declaration of nullity on the ground of ignorance of carnal copulation, the ecclesiastical tribunal upheld the validity of the marriage in view of the non-essential character of carnal copulation, indicating that since carnal copulation did not constitute a substantial element of the marriage contract, ignorance of carnal copulation did not vitiate the consent of the parties. Thus the Sacred Congregation of the Council in reviewing a case brought on appeal from the Archdiocese of Bamberg, in which a woman protested that she had no idea of the physical use of marriage, declared that ignorance of carnal copulation had no bearing on the validity of the marriage contract.[25] Similarly the Roman Rota indicated that knowledge of carnal copulation was not necessary for the instituting of a valid marriage contract. It upheld the validity of marriages which were questioned on the ground of ignorance regarding carnal copulation.[26]

Although carnal copulation in itself is not necessary for perfecting the marriage contract, it is not absolutely removed from the essential sphere of marriage. Carnal copulation may be said to be essential to the act of contracting marriage by reason of the right from which it flows, inasmuch as the right to carnal

24 Sanchez, *De Sancto Matrimonii Sacramento*, lib. II, disp. XXVII, n. 3, quoted by S. C. C. *in Csanadien.*, 18 dec. 1869 — *Thesaurus*, CXXVIII (1869), 672.

25 Pallottini, *s. v. Matrimonium*, III, *Quoad consensum*, n. 6.

26 S. R. R., *Nullitatis Matrimonii*, 17 mart. 1910, coram R. P. D. Iosepho Mori, dec. XII — *S. R. R. Decisiones*, II (1910), 117; S. R. R., *Nullitatis Matrimonii*, 20 ian. 1926, coram R. P. D. Iulio Grazioli, dec. II — *S. R. R. Decisiones*, XVIII (1926), 4-11; S. R. R., *Nullitatis Matrimonii*, 17 mart. 1926, coram R. P. D. Andrea Jullien, dec. X — *S. R. R. Decisiones*, XVIII (1926), 68-75.

copulation does constitute a substantial element of the marriage contract.[27] Consequently a person who contracts marriage must will to concede the right to carnal copulation explicitly or implicitly. The explicit will to concede the right to carnal copulation is founded on clear knowledge of what carnal copulation is. The implicit will does not require such a clearly defined notion of carnal copulation. It suffices that the contracting parties know in general that they are conceding and accepting a corporal right for the performance of acts ordained for the procreation of children.[28] By knowingly conceding the corporal right to the performance of acts destined by nature for the procreation of children, the parties are implicitly willing to concede the right to carnal copulation, even though their actual knowledge gives no specification to the acts so ordained other than that they are the object of a corporal right, and therefore necessarily corporal acts.[29] In knowingly conceding the right to the performance of corporal acts in general, a person may, for the purposes of a valid matrimonial consent, rightly be said to will to concede the right to carnal copulation.

The necessity for the intellectual determination of the acts which are the object of the conjugal right as corporal acts is implied by canon 1082, §1. This canon states that the parties to a marriage contract must know that marriage is a society. Knowledge of marriage as a society implies by law knowledge that involves co-operation as determined by the conjugal right

27 "Dicendum est consensum matrimonium constituentem non esse explicite in carnalem copulam, sed in ius et potestatem ad talem copulam, quia carnalis copula non est de matrimonii essentia, sed eius effectus et operatio." — Sanchez, *op. cit.*, lib. II, disp. XXVII, n. 3; S. C. C., *in Csanadien.*, 18 dec. 1869 — *Thesaurus*, CXXVIII (1869), 672.

28 The concession and the acceptance of the corporal right to the performance of acts which serve the purpose of procreation is the essential object of the matrimonial consent (canon 1081, §2), and consequently the object of necessary knowledge.

29 "Ius ad ipsam [copulam carnalem] tradi et accipi satis implicite cognosci et in consensu comprehendi potest ab eo qui non ignorat, ex cooperatione utriusque coniugis filios procreari et ad hoc matrimonium ordinari." — Wernz-Vidal, *Ius Matrimoniale*, n. 457, ad annot. 13.

on which the conjugal society is founded.[30] But co-operation in accordance with the conjugal right, which in the contemplation of the law is essentially a corporal right,[31] is equivalent to corporal co-operation, which in practice is reduced to the performance of corporal acts.

A further indication that it is necessary for a person who contracts marriage to know that he is conceding the right to the performance of corporal acts is derived from a consideration of the essential object of the matrimonial consent. The essential object of a matrimonial consent consists in the concession and acceptance of a right to the married partner's body for the purpose of performing acts *(in ordine ad actus)*. The object of the consent, therefore, is not simply the concession and acceptance of the right to the body, but the concession and acceptance of the right to the body for the performance of acts, acts which are the object of the right to the body, and which, inasmuch as they proceed from the right to the body, are specified as corporal acts.

From what has been said one may directly infer that the intellectual determination of the corporal act need not extend to an understanding of the mode of carnal copulation.[32] It suffices that the parties to the marriage contract know that to secure the end for which their union is instituted there must be had some corporal union *(concursus corporum)* or corporal familiarity.[33] Consequently, a person would contract a valid marriage if he believed that the procreation of children was effected by a chaste embrace, a kiss, or even the linking of arms, as long as he did not exclude positively all but these actions when he gave his consent for marriage. For a person who gives his consent for

30 Wernz-Vidal, *Ius Matrimoniale,* n. 547; Payen, *De Matrimonio in Missionibus,* III, nn. 1623-1626.

31 Cf. canon 1081, §2.

32 Chelodi, *Ius Matrimoniale,* n. 110; Cappello, *De Matrimonio,* n. 582; Gougnard, *op. cit.,* p. 150; Blat, *Commentarium Textus Codicis Iuris Canonici* (5 vols. in 6, Romae, 1919-1927), Vol. III, pars I, p. 613.

33 Wernz-Vidal, *op. cit.,* n. 457; Vermeersch-Creusen, *op. cit.,* Vol. II, n. 369; Payen, *op. cit.,* III, p. 253, n. 1623-1626; Claeys-Bouuaert—Simenon, *Manuale Iuris Canonici* (3 vols., Vol. II, *De Sacramentis,* Gandae et Leodii, 1931), II, *De Sacramentis,* n. 287; Chelodi, *loc. cit.*

marriage even with such an erroneous opinion is still obliging himself to corporal co-operation for the procreation of children.[34]

From what has been said thus far concerning the knowledge required for the eliciting of a valid matrimonial consent, it may be concluded that ignorance vitiates the consent of the parties to a marriage contract when they do not know that in giving their consent for marriage they are giving over a corporal right and thereby taking upon themselves the obligation of corporal co-operation, which involves specifically the performance of corporal acts or corporal familiarity *(concursus corporum)*. Consequently, if a person contracts marriage, believing that the consent of the parties and the consequent perfection of the contract give rise to the spontaneous generation of children without any intervening activity or co-operation on the part of the principals, or if they believe that through the formation of the contract they become eligible to receive children, which in their estimation are presented to married couples by a physician, or indeed are beset by any similar notion which may be commonly employed as a cloak to safeguard innocence, they are not in possession of a sufficient knowledge to give a valid consent to marry.

Similarly, if a man or woman believes that the procreation of children is exclusively the work of a woman, so that the idea of co-operation to secure the end of marriage has no place in his or her understanding of marriage, such a person is in ignorance of the object of the nature of the marriage contract, and does not elicit a valid matrimonial consent. Again, if the parties to a marriage contract have a general idea that children are begotten through their corporate activity, but do not realize that they concede the right and consequently are obliged to corporal co-

34 Cappello and Gougnard, believing that the proper and specific object of the matrimonial consent must be determined by at least an obscure knowledge of carnal copulation, deny that a valid matrimonial consent can be elicited by one who thinks that generation results from a kiss. However, they concede that the mode of generation is not the object of necessary knowledge. It is difficult to see how they can reconcile the two ideas. — Cappello, *loc. cit.;* Gougnard, *loc. cit.*

operation involving corporal familiarity, their consent is invalid on the ground of ignorance.

When the validity of a matrimonial consent is impugned on the ground of ignorance regarding any aspect of the essential object of the marriage contract, such ignorance must be conclusively proved. The statement of the parties, namely, that they would not have given their consent to marry had they known that they were obliging themselves to have carnal intercourse, has no probative force in canonical procedure.[35] Such a statement on their part implies nothing more than an interpretative intention. But that kind of intention has no place in the real order of things.[36]

In practice, when ignorance is said to exist and revolve around the notion of carnal intercourse, either the ignorant party refuses to have intercourse, in which case a person may avail himself of the legal remedy of a dispensation from a non-consummated marriage, or he willingly performs the conjugal act, and thereby ratifies a possibly defective consent. If an ignorant person is forced to have intercourse, he or she may resort to a legal action to secure a declaration of nullity, in which case it must be evident that the person did not know that matrimonial consent entailed an obligation to co-operate corporally for the procreation of children.[37]

Article II — Ignorance of the Ends of Marriage

The conjugal society, the union of a man and a woman founded on the mutual concession and acceptance of the corporal right, is ordained by nature for the procreation of children. The

35 Gasparri, *op. cit.*, II, 901; Cerato, *Matrimonium a Codice Iuris Canonici Integre Desumptum* (4. ed., Patavii, 1927), n. 78; Chelodi, *Ius Matrimoniale*, n. 110.

36 "Intentio interpretativa est de illa quam homo numquam habuit, est tamen ita comparatus animo, ut eam haberet, si de ea cogitaret." — Ferraris, *Prompta Bibliotheca, Canonica, Iuridica, Moralis, Theologica, necnon Ascetica, Polemica, Rubricistica, Historica* (9 vols., Romae, 1885-1899), IV, s. v. *Intentio.*

37 Chelodi, *op. cit.*, n. 110; Cerato, *op. cit.*, n. 78.

natural effect of the corporal co-operation which is the object of the conjugal right is the generation of children.[38] Canon 1082, §1, declares that the validity of a matrimonial consent requires that a man and a woman in contracting marriage know that the procreation of children is the primary end of their union.[39] They may have in mind any honorable reason or motive for the contracting of marriage with a particular person, such as the securing of riches, the enhancement of family honor, or the nurturing of their mutual affection,[40] but they must know that marriage, by the will of the Author of nature Himself, has as its primary end the procreation of children.

The procreation of children must be recognized as the end of marriage, even though the contracting parties know and will any other end that is intrinsic and essential to marriage.[41] If a spouse believed that the end of marriage consists exclusively in mutual aid and companionship, he or she would not elicit a valid matrimonial consent.[42] Again, if the contracting parties have the will to form a union in order that they may have a legitimate way for satisfying the sex appetite, and have even specific knowledge of the corporal acts which effect the generation of offspring, but at the same time do not know that the generation

38 "Veritas huius asserti (nempe, matrimonii finis primarius est procreatio prolis) eruitur ex absoluta actus coniugalis necessitate eiusque aptitudine ut proles procreatur." — Vermeersch-Creusen, *Epitome Iuris Canonici*, II, n. 275.

39 "Ut matrimonialis consensus haberi possit, necesse est ut contrahentes saltem non ignorent matrimonium esse societatem permanentem inter virum et mulierem ad filios procreandos."

40 Vermeersch-Creusen, *loc. cit.;* Wernz-Vidal, *Ius Matrimoniale*, n. 26.

41 Payen, *De Matrimonio in Missionibus*, III, n. 1623-1626.

42 The Roman Rota declared a marriage invalid when it was proved that the union was formed for the exclusive purpose of social convenience. A certain Leonard Waern married Mary Hoogland in order that he might have a woman to assume the duties of a hostess in his home. Mary Hoogland, in her turn, agreed to the union, intending only to take upon herself the duties of a housekeeper. The decision of the Rota indicated that the will of the parties was not such as to constitute a matrimonial consent. — S. R. R., *Nullitatis Matrimonii*, 19 aug. 1914, coram R. P. D. Aloysio Sincero, dec. XXIX — *S. R. R. Decisiones*, V (1914), 307-312.

of offspring is the natural effect of their corporal acts, they do not according to canon 1082, §1, furnish a valid consent for marriage. Even the belief that the education of the children — as closely allied as it is to the idea of procreation — is the end for which the conjugal union is instituted does not suffice for the giving of a valid matrimonial consent, if the parties do not know that children are begotten of marriage itself. As long as a man or a woman does not associate the procreation of children with the marriage contract, he or she does not have the requisite knowledge to elicit a matrimonial consent.

The fact that the actual generation of children is impossible has no effect on the required knowledge as provided for by canon 1082, §1. Elderly persons as well as persons who are sterile must know that marriage is a society between a man and a woman for the procreation of children, even though the procreation of children constitutes an end that can never be realized in their particular case. The fact, too, that parties to a marriage contract would have willed to marry had they known that the procreation of children represented the primary end of marriage can in no way render their consent valid.[43] An interpretative intention has no place in the order of reality. It can neither destroy the validity of a consent when it is founded on knowledge that is not essential to the contract, nor can it ratify an invalid consent when it deals with necessary knowledge.

The Code makes no specific reference to the education of the children or to the secondary ends of marriage, namely the mutual aid and the remedy for concupiscence, in its declaration concerning the requisite knowledge for the eliciting of a valid matrimonial consent. However, if a person has knowledge of all the elements contained in canon 1082, §1, he cannot but know that marriage is further ordained for the education of the children, for the exchange of mutual aid, and as a remedy for concupiscence. Because of the necessary connection between the procreation and the education of children, a person could not know that marriage is ordained for the procreation of children without realizing at the same time that the obligation of educating chil-

43 Gasparri, *Tractatus Canonicus de Matrimonio,* II, n. 901.

dren pertained to the marriage state. Then, too, one who is familiar with the concept of society, comprehending as it does the note of co-operation, necessarily knows that the purpose of marriage is to provide mutual aid for the spouses. Finally, when a person knows that the marriage contract involves the giving and accepting of a right to the married partner's body for the performance of corporal acts, he must realize that marriage offers a legitimate way to obtain relief from carnal concupiscence.

Article III — Ignorance of the Properties of Marriage

Canon 1082, §1, further declares that the ambit of requisite knowledge for the eliciting of a valid matrimonial consent includes the notes of unity and indissolubility. In the words of the canon the contracting parties must know that marriage is a society between one man and one woman *(virum et mulierem)*, and they must know that it is a permanent society. Consequently, if a person ignorant of the unity and permanence of matrimony contracts marriage with the idea that he may concede the corporal right to another, so that the right to his body may be shared simultaneously by two or more persons, he does not give a valid consent to marry; or if a person enters into a marriage contract thinking that the duration of the marriage bond is determined by the will of the parties themselves to be husband and wife, so that when the will to be married ceases the marriage bond likewise ceases to exist, neither his consent nor the consequent state can be termed matrimonial.[44]

Ignorance of the essential properties of marriage must not be confused with simple error regarding them. Ignorance of itself pertains to ideas, whereas error is referred to judgments.[45] When a person is ignorant of the properties of marriage he has no idea of the permanent and exclusive nature of the marriage bond; but the very fact that he is in error indicates that he has associated the ideas of permanence and exclusiveness with the marriage

44 Cf. Cerato, *Matrimonium a Codice Iuris Canonici Integre Desumptum*, n. 78.

45 Cerato, *ibidem*, n. 79.

contract, for in the judgment by which he arrived at his erroneous belief he has compared or contrasted permanence with non-permanence, unity with plurality.[46]

Thus the fact that a person contracts marriage with the erroneous belief that he can, while his marriage bond still exists, have marital relations with anyone other than his spouse, or the fact that he believes that his marriage bond can be dissolved by civil law, does not necessarily imply that he is ignorant of the fact that marriage is a permanent society between a man and a woman for the procreation of children.[47] For this reason simple error, while it remains in the purely speculative stage, that is, as long as it does not constitute a *conditio sine qua non* or reflect a positive act of the will contrary to the essential properties of marriage, does not affect the validity of a matrimonial consent.[48] Ignorance, on the other hand, since it implies the complete absence of any will either implicit or explicit for the forming of an exclusive and permanent union, does render the matrimonial consent invalid.[49]

46 Dubray, *Introductory Philosophy*, p. 117.

47 Farrugia, *De Matrimonio et Causis Matrimonialibus* (Taurini-Romae, 1924), n. 28.

48 Cf. canons 1084, 1092, 3°; 1086, §2.

49 Cf. canon 1082, §1.

CONCLUSIONS

1. Prior to the Council of Trent legislation concerning the effect of ignorance on matrimonial consent was referred almost exclusively to cases involving persons in whom mental activity was impossible or at least impaired. (pp. 11-12)

2. The age of the Decretalists saw the inauguration of a scientific study concerning ignorance in relation to marriage, particularly in connection with legislation determining the requisite age for marriage. However, it was not until the middle of the nineteenth century that the extent of the ignorance which sufficed to invalidate a matrimonial consent was explicitly determined in ecclesiastical law. (pp. 11-12, 22, 23, 27)

3. Mental incapacity affects the validity of the marriage contract only when it is coincident with the time when the consent is given. (p. 46)

4. The degree of deliberation required for the commission of a mortal sin may be used as a norm in the reaching of a judgment regarding the ability of those who are semi-insane, intoxicated, or drugged to contract marriage, but only if such persons possessed the necessary discretion and knowledge to elicit a valid matrimonial consent while in their normal state of mind. (pp. 50-53, 63-65)

5. A person who is so intoxicated that he is capable only of placing the voluntary act by which he formally expresses his will to contract marriage, marries validly only by reason of a virtual consent. (p. 64)

6. An insane person cannot contract marriage in virtue of the continuance of a previous consent. Consequently, a marriage that was invalid by reason of a diriment impediment cannot be convalidated or radically sanated if at the time of the proposed convalidation or radical sanation a person is insane. However, if the mental state is effected by an incidental cause, such as intoxication or somnambulism, a convalidation or radical sanation can be had. (pp. 66-69)

7. The age of discretion relative to marriage is coincident with the age of puberty. (pp. 70-71)

8. There is no necessary connection between the age of discretion and the physical or legal age of puberty. Puberty is associated with discretion only because puberty is reached at an age when the intellectual faculty is believed to have had sufficient time to develop. A person may be endowed with the necessary discretion to contract marriage before puberty, or he may lack sufficient discretion after attaining to puberty. (pp. 72-75)

9. A person is not devoid of the necessary knowledge to give his consent for the contracting of marriage if he knows that the marriage contract involves the mutual concession of a permanent and exclusive right to corporal co-operation for the procreation of children. (pp. 77-79)

10. Knowledge of carnal copulation is not required for the validity of a matrimonial consent. It suffices that the contracting parties know that they are obliging themselves to the performance of corporal acts. (pp. 82-86)

BIBLIOGRAPHY

SOURCES

Acta Apostolicae Sedis, Commentarium Officiale, Romae, 1909 —.

Acta Sanctae Sedis, 41 vols., Romae, 1865-1908.

Bullarum Diplomatum et Privilegiorum Sanctorum Romanorum Pontificum Taurinensis Editio, 24 vols. et 2 Appendices, Augustae Taurinorum-Neapoli, 1857-1885.

Codex Iuris Canonici Pii X Pontificis Maximi iussu digestus Benedicti Papae XV auctoritate promulgatus, Romae: Typis Polyglottis Vaticanis, 1917.

Codicis Iuris Canonici Fontes cura Emi. Petri Card. Gasparri editi, 9 vols., Romae (postea in Civitate Vaticana), Typis Polyglottis Vaticanis, 1923-1929. Vols. VII-IX, ed. cura et studio Emi. Iustiniani Card. Serédi).

Collectanea S. Congregationis de Propaganda Fide, 2 vols., Romae: Typographia Polyglotta S. C. de Propaganda Fide, 1907.

Corpus Iuris Canonici, ed. Lipsiensis 2., post Aemilii L. Richteri curas instruxit Aemilius Friedberg, 2 vols., Lipsiae: Ex Officina Bernhardi Tauchnitz, 1879-1881. Ed. anastatice repetita, Lipsiae: Tauchnitz, 1928.

Corpus Iuris Civilis, Digesta Justiniani Augusti — recognoverunt et ediderunt P. Bonfante, C. Fadda, C. Ferrini, S. Riccobono, V. Scialoia, Mediolani: Società Editrice Libraria, 1931.

Decretum Gratiani emendatum et Notationibus illustratum una cum Glossis, Romae, 1582.

Decretales D. Gregorii IX, una cum glossis restitutae, Romae, 1582.

Fontes Iuris Romani Antejustiniani — ediderunt S. Riccobono, J. Baviera, C. Ferrini, Florentiae: apud G. Barbera, 1908.

Jaffe, Philippus, *Regesta Pontificum Romanorum ab condita Ecclesia ad annum post Christum natum MCXCVIII,* 2. ed. cura Wattenbach, Kaltenbrunner, Edwald, Loewenfeld, 2 vols., Lipsiae, 1885-1888.

Mansi, Ioannes, *Sacrorum Conciliorum Nova et Amplissima Collectio,* 53 vols. in 60, Parisiis Arnhem-Leipzig, 1901-1927.

Pallottini, S., *Collectio omnium conclusionum et resolutionum quae in causis propositis apud Sacram Congregationem Cardinalium S. Concilii Tridentini interpretum prodierunt et eius institutione anno MDLXIV ad MDCCCLX, distinctis titulis alphabetico ordine per materias digesta,* 18 vols., Romae, 1868-1893.

Potthast, Augustus, *Regesta Pontificum Romanorum inde ab anno post Christum natum MCXCVIII ad annum MCCCIV,* 2 vols., Berolini, 1874-1875.

Sacrae Romanae Rotae Decisiones seu Sententiae (ab anno 1909), Romae: Typis Vaticanis, 1912 —.

Sacra Romanae Rotae Decisiones coram R. P. D. Francisco Buratti, Romae, 1624.

Thesaurus Resolutionum Sacrae Congregationis Concilii, 167 vols., Romae, 1718-1908.

Vignali, Giovanni, *Corpo del Diritto, corredato delle note di Dionisio Golofredo e di C. E. Freiesleben, altrimento Ferromontano*, 8 vols., Napoli, 1859.

Reference Works

Augustine, Charles, *A Commentary on the New Code of Canon Law*, 8 vols., St. Louis, 1918-1921. Vol. V., revised edition, 1920.

Ayrinhac, H. A. - Lydon, P. J., *Marriage Legislation in the New Code of Canon Law*, revised edition, New York: Benziger Brothers, 1940.

Barbossa, Augustinus, *Collectanea Doctorum tam Veterum quam Recentiorum in Ius Pontificium Universum*, 5 vols., Lugduni, 1637.

Blat, A., *Commentarium Textus Codicis Iuris Canonici*, 5 vols. in 6, Romae, 1919-1927.

Boich, Henricus, *Commentaria in Quinque Decretalium Libros*, Venetiis, 1576.

Cappello, Felix M., *Tractatus Canonico-Moralis de Sacramentis*, Vols. I, III, 4. ed. emendata et aucta, Augustae Taurinorum et Romae, 1939.

Cerato, P., *Matrimonium a Codice Iuris Canonici Integre Desumptum*, 4. ed., Patavii, Libr. Gregoriare Editi. Typis Seminarii, 1927.

Chelodi, Ioannes, *Ius Matrimoniale iuxta Codicem Iuris Canonici*, 3. ed., Tridenti Libr. Edit. Tridentum, 1921.

Claeys Bouuaert, F. - Simenon, G., *Manuale Iuris Canonici*, 3 vols., Vols. I, III in 3. ed., 1930, Vol. II in 1. ed., 1931, *De Sacramentis*, Gandae et Leodii: Dessain, 1931.

Covarrubias y Leyva, Didacus, *Opera Omnia* (2 vols., Coloniae Allobrogum, 1679).

D'Annibale, I., *Summula Theologiae Moralis*, 5. ed., 3 vols., Romae, 1908.

De Becker, Iulius, *De Sponsalibus et Matrimonio Praelectiones Canonicae*, 2. ed., Lovanii, New York, 1903.

De Lugo, Ioannes, *Disputationes Scholasticae et Morales*, 8 vols., Parisiis, 1869.

Doheny, William, *Canonical Procedure in Matrimonial Cases*, Milwaukee: The Bruce Publishing Company, 1938.

Dorcus, Roy Melvin - Shaffer, George Wilson, *Textbook of Abnormal Psychology*, 1 ed., Williams & Wilkins: Baltimore, 1934.

Dubray, Charles A., *Introductory Philosophy*, New York: Longmans, Green & Co., 1933.

Esser, Gerardus, *Psychologia*, Techny, Ill.: Typis Domus Missionum ad St. Mariam, 1931.

Fagnanus, Prosper, *Commentaria in Quinque Libros Decretalium*, 4 vols., Romae, 1661.

Farrugia, Nicolaus, *De Matrimonio et Causis Matrimonialibus*, Taurini-Romae, 1924.

Ferraris, Lucius, *Prompta Bibliotheca, Canonica, Iuridica, Moralis, Theologica, necnon Ascetica, Polemica, Rubricistica, Historica*, 9 vols., Romae, 1885-1891.

Ford, John C., *The Validity of Virginal Marriage*, Worcester, Mass.: Harrigan Press, 1938.

Fourneret, Pierre, *Le Mariage Chrêten*, Paris, 1919.

Gasparri, Petrus, *Tractatus Canonicus de Matrimonio*, 3. ed., 2 vols., Parisiis, 1904.

Gonzales-Tellez, Emmanuel, *Commentaria Perpetua in Singulos Textus Quinque Librorum Decretalium Gregorii IX*, 5 vols. in 4, Lugduni, 1715.

Gougnard, Armandus, *Tractatus de Matrimonio*, 7. ed., Mechliniae: H. Dessain, 1931.

Hickey, J. S., *Summula Philosophiae Scholasticae*, 3 vols., St. Louis: Herder & Co., Vol. I, 8. ed., 1933; Vol. II, 7. ed., 1927; Vol. III, 7. ed., 1934.

Hilling, Nicholas, *Procedure at the Roman Curia*, a translation published by J. F. Wagner, New York, 1907.

Hostiensis, Cardinalis (Henricus de Segusia), *Commentaria in Quinque Decretalium Libros*, 5 vols. in 3, Venetiis, 1581.

Joyce, George, *Christian Marriage*, London and New York, 1933.

Knecht, August, *Handbuch des katholischen Eherechts*, Freiburg im Breisgau: Herder, 1928.

Lanza, Antonius, *Theologia Moralis Specialis de Matrimonio*, Romae, 1940.

Lehmkuhl Augustinus, *Theologia Moralis*, 5. ed., 2 vols., Friburgi Brisgoviae, 1888.

Leurenius, Petrus, *Ius Canonicum Universum*, 3 vols., Venettis, 1729.

Macksey, J., *De Ethica Naturali*, Romae, 1914.

Manning, John Joseph, *Presumption of Law in Matrimonial Procedure*, The Catholic University of America Canon Law Studies, n. 94, Washington, D. C.: The Catholic University of America, 1935.

Migne, Jacque Paul, *Patrologiae Cursus Completus, Series Latina*, 221 vols., Parisiis, 1844-1864.

Murray, Raymond W., *Introductory Sociology*, New York: F. S. Crofts & Co., 1936.

Noldin, H. - Schmitt, A., *Summa Theologiae Moralis*, 3 vols., Oeniponte: Typis et Sumptibus Fel. Rauch, 1938-1940. Vol. III, 26. ed., 1940.

Palmieri, Dominicus, *Tractatus de Matrimonio*, Romae: Typis Polyglottis, 1880.

Panormitanus, Abbas (Nicolaus de Tudeschis), *Commentaria in Quinque Libros Decretalium*, 5 vols. in 7, 1588.

Payen, G., *De Matrimonio in Missionibus ac potissimum in Sinis Tractatus Practicus et Casus*, 2. ed., 3 vols., Zi-ka-wei: Typographia T'OU-SE-WE, 1935-1936.

Petrus Lombardus Libri IV Sententiarum (2. ed., 2 vols., ad claras aquas ex typographis Collegii S. Bonaventurae, 1916), II, 917, 918, 921.

Pirhing, Ernricus, *Ius Canonicum Nova Methodo Explicatum*, 5 vols. in 4, Dilingae, 1674-1678.

Pontius, Basilius, *De Sacramento Matrimonii Tractatus cum appendice de matrimonio Catholici cum heretico*, Bruxellis, 1627.

Prümmer, Dominicus M., *Manuale Theologiae Moralis*, 3 vols., Friburgi Brisgoviae: Herder & Co., Vol. III, 4. et 5. ed., 1928.

Reiffenstuel, Anacletus, *Ius Canonicum Universum*, 7 vols., Parisiis, 1864-1870.

Rufinus, *Summa Decretorium*, ed. Singer, Paderborn, 1902.

Sanchez, Thomas, *De Sancto Matrimonii Sacramento*, 3 vols. in 2, Antverpiae, 1607.

Schmalzgrueber, Franciscus, *Jus Ecclesiasticum Universum*, 5 vols. in 12, Romae, 1843-1845.

Thomas Aquinas, St., *Summa Theologica*, diligenter emendata, Nicolai, Sylvii, Billuart et C. J. Drioux notis ornata, 6. ed., 8 vols., Barri-Ducis, 1870.

——, *Opera Omnia*, studio ac labore Stanislai Frette et Pauli Mare, 34 vols., Parisiis: Apud L. Vivès, 1871-1880.

Vermeersch, Arthurus, *Theologiae Moralis Principia, Responsa, Consilia*, 3. ed., 4 vols., Romae, 1933-1937.

Vermeersch, A. - Creusen, J., *Epitome Iuris Canonici*, 3 vols., Mechliniae-Romae, Vol. II, 5. ed., 1934.

Vlaming, Th. M., *Praelectiones Iuris Matrimonii ad Normam Codicis Iuris Canonici*, 3. ed., 2 vols., Bussum in Hollandia, 1919-1921.

Wernz, Franciscus, *Ius Decretalium*, 2. ed., 6 vols., Romae et Prati, 1906-1913.

Wernz, F. - Vidal, P., *Ius Canonicum*, 7 vols. in 8, Romae: Apud Aedes Universitatis Gregorianae, 1927-1938. Vol. V, *Ius Matrimoniale*, 2. ed., 1928.

Wex, Iacobus, *Ariadne Carolino-Canonica, Doctrina Theoretico-practica SS. Canonum*, Dilingae, 1708.

Woywod, Stanislaus, *A Practical Commentary on the Code of Canon Law*, 5. ed., 2 vols., New York: Joseph F. Wagner, Inc., 1939.

Articles

Anonymous, "De Cognitione Aestimativa in Matrimonio." — *Periodica de Re Morali, Canonica, Liturgica*, XXX (1941), 5-19.

Oesterle, Gerardus, "Nullitas Matrimonii ex Capite Ignorantiae." — *Ephemerides Theologicae Lovanienses*, XV (1938), 547 sq.

PERIODICALS

Periodica de Re Canonica et Morali utili praesertim Religiosis et Missionariis, Brugis, 1905 —; from the year 1927: *Periodica de Re Canonica, Morali, Liturgica.*

Ephemerides Theologicae Lovanienses, Lovanii, Universitas Catholica Lovaniensis, 1924 —.

ABBREVIATIONS

AAS — *Acta Apostolicae Sedis.*

Fontes — *Codicis Iuris Canonici Fontes cura . . . Gasaprri editi.*

Jaffé — *Regesta Pontificum Romanorum* (edited by Kaltenbrunner, Ewald, Loewenfeld).

Mansi — *Sacrorum Conciliorum Nova et Amplissima Collectio.*

Pallottini — *Collectio Omnium Conclusionum et Resolutionum*, etc.

Potthast — *Regesta Pontificum Romanorum.*

S. C. C. — Sacra Congregatio Concilii.

S. C. S. Off. — Suprema Congregatio Sancti Officii.

S. R. R. — Sacra Romana Rota.

ANALYTICAL INDEX

BIOGRAPHICAL NOTE

Vincent Michael Smith was born on July 25, 1918, in Philadelphia, Pennsylvania. He attended St. Michael's and Incarnation Parochial Schools and Northeast Catholic High School of that city. In September of 1934 he was admitted into the Seminary of St. Charles Borromeo, Philadelphia, where he completed his preparatory studies and his course in Philosophy. In July of 1939 he was sent to pursue his theological studies at the Pontifical Roman Seminary, Rome, Italy. The following year he entered the Theological College of the Catholic University of America, where he received the degree of Licentiate in Sacred Theology in May, 1943. He was ordained to the Holy Priesthood on May 29, 1943, at Philadelphia. In the fall of that year he enrolled in the School of Canon Law of the Catholic University of America, from which he received the degree of Baccalaureate in Canon Law in May of 1944, and the degree of Licentiate in Canon Law in May, 1945.

CANON LAW STUDIES*

1. FRERIKS, REV. CELESTINE A., C.PP.S., J.C.D., Religious Congregations in Their External Relations, 121 pp., 1916.
2. GALLIHER, REV. DANIEL M., O.P., J.C.D., Canonical Elections, 117 pp., 1917.
3. BORKOWSKI, REV. AURELIUS L., O.F.M., J.C.D., De Confraternitatibus Ecclesiasticis, 136 pp., 1918.
4. CASTILLO, REV. CAYO, J.C.D., Disertacion Historico-Canonica sobre la Potestad del Cabildo en Sede Vacante o Impedida del Vicario Capitular, 99 pp., 1919 (1918).
5. KUBELBECK, REV. WILLIAM J., S.T.B., J.C.D., The Sacred Penitentiaria and Its Relation to Faculties of Ordinaries and Priests, 129 pp., 1918.
6. PETROVITS, REV. JOSEPH, J.C., S.T.D., J.C.D., The New Church Law on Matrimony, X-461 pp., 1919.
7. HICKEY, REV. JOHN J., S.T.B., J.C.D., Irregularities and Simple Impediments in the New Code of Canon Law, 100 pp., 1920.
8. KLEKOTKA, REV. PETER J., S.T.B., J.C.D., Diocesan Consultors, 179 pp., 1920.
9. WANENMACHER, REV. FRANCIS, J.C.D., The Evidence in Ecclesiastical Procedure Affecting the Marriage Bond, 1920 (Printed 1935).
10. GOLDEN, REV. HENRY FRANCIS, J.C.D., Parochial Benefices in the New Code, IV-119 pp., 1921 (Printed 1925).
11. KOUDELKA, REV. CHARLES J., J.C.D., Pastors, Their Rights and Duties According to the New Code of Canon Law, 211 pp., 1921.
12. MELO, REV. ANTONIUS, O.F.M., J.C.D., De Exemptione Regularium, X-188 pp., 1921.
13. SCHAAF, REV. VALENTINE THEODORE, O.F.M., S.T.B., J.C.D., The Cloister, X-180 pp., 1921.
14. BURKE, REV. THOMAS JOSEPH, S.T.D., J.C.D., Competence in Ecclesiastical Tribunals, IV-117 pp., 1922.
15. LEECH, REV. GEORGE LEO, J.C.D., A Comparative Study of the Constitution "Apostolicae Sedis" and the "Codex Juris Canonici," 179 pp., 1922.
16. MOTRY, REV. HUBERT LOUIS, S.T.D., J.C.D., Diocesan Faculties According to the Code of Canon Law, II-167 pp., 1922.
17. MURPHY, REV. GEORGE LAWRENCE, J.C.D., Delinquencies and Penalties in the Administration and the Reception of the Sacraments, IV-121 pp., 1923.

* From nn. 1-100 inclusive only n. 25 is still obtainable.
From n. 101 onward all numbers are available except the following: nn. 101-114 inclusive; also nn. 116, 118, 120, 122, 123 and 162.

18. O'Reilly, Rev. John Anthony, S.T.B., J.C.D., Ecclesiastical Sepulture in the New Code of Canon Law, II-129 pp., 1923.
19. Michalicka, Rev. Wenceslas Cyril, O.S.B., J.C.D., Judicial Procedure in Dismissal of Clerical Exempt Religious, 107 pp., 1923.
20. Dargin, Rev. Edward Vincent, S.T.B., J.C.D., Reserved Cases According to the Code of Canon Law, IV-103 pp., 1924.
21. Godfrey, Rev. John A., S.T.B., J.C.D., The Right of Patronage According to the Code of Canon Law, 153 pp., 1924.
22. Hagedorn, Rev. Francis Edward, J.C.D., General Legislation on Indulgences, II-154 pp., 1924.
23. King, Rev. James Ignatius, J.C.D., The Administration of the Sacraments to Dying Non-Catholics, V-141 pp., 1924.
24. Winslow, Rev. Francis Joseph, O.F.M., J.C.D., Vicars and Prefects Apostolic, IV-149 pp., 1924.
25. Correa, Rev. Jose Servelion, S.T.L., J.C.D., La Potestad Legislativa de la Iglesia Catolica, IV-127 pp., 1925.
26. Dugan, Rev. Henry Francis, A.M., J.C.D., The Judiciary Department of the Diocesan Curia, 87 pp., 1925.
27. Keller, Rev. Charles Frederick, S.T.B., J.C.D., Mass Stipends, 167 pp., 1925.
28. Paschang, Rev. John Linus, J.C.D., The Sacramentals According to the Code of Canon Law, 129 pp., 1925.
29. Piontek, Rev. Cyrillus, O.F.M., S.T.B., J.C.D., De Indulto Exclaustrationis necnon Saecularizationis, XIII-289 pp., 1925.
30. Kearney, Rev. Richard Joseph, S.T.B., J.C.D., Sponsors at Baptism According to the Code of Canon Law, IV-127 pp. 1925.
31. Bartlett, Rev. Chester Joseph, A.M., LL.B., J.C.D., The Tenure of Parochial Property in the United States of America, V-108 pp., 1926.
32. Kilker, Rev. Adrian Jerome, J.C.D., Extreme Unction, V-425 pp., 1926.
33. McCormick, Rev. Robert Emmet, J.C.D., Confessors of Religious, VIII-266 pp., 1926.
34. Miller, Rev. Newton Thomas, J.C.D., Founded Masses According to the Code of Canon Law, VII-93 pp., 1926.
35. Roelker, Rev. Edward G., S.T.D., J.C.D., Principles of Privilege According to the Code of Canon Law, XI-166 pp., 1926.
36. Bakalarczyk, Rev. Richardus, M.I.C., J.U.D., De Novitiatu, VIII-208 pp., 1927.
37. Pizzuti, Rev. Lawrence, O.F.M., J.U.L., De Parochis Religiosis, 1927. (Not Printed).
38. Bliley, Rev. Nicholas Martin, O.S.B., J.C.D., Altars According to the Code of Canon Law, XIX-132 pp., 1927.

39. Brown, Mr. Brendan Francis, A.B., LL.M., J.U.D., The Canonical Juristic Personality with Special Reference to its Status in the United States of America, V-212 pp., 1927.
40. Cavanaugh, Rev. William Thomas, C.P., J.U.D., The Reservation of the Blessed Sacrament, VIII-101 pp., 1927.
41. Doheny, Rev. William J., C.S.C., A.B., J.U.D., Church Property: Modes of Acquisition, X-118 pp., 1927.
42. Feldhaus, Rev. Aloysius H., C.PP.S., J.C.D., Oratories, IX-141 pp., 1927.
43. Kelly, Rev. James Patrick, A.B., J.C.D., The Jurisdiction of the Simple Confessor, X-208 pp., 1927.
44. Neuberger, Rev. Nicholas J., J.C.D., Canon 6 or the Relation of the Codex Juris Canonici to the Preceding Legislation, V-95 pp., 1927.
45. O'Keefe, Rev. Gerald Michael, J.C.D., Matrimonial Dispensations, Powers of Bishops, Priests, and Confessors, VIII-232 pp., 1927.
46. Quigley, Rev. Joseph A. M., A.B., J.C.D., Condemned Societies, 139 pp., 1927.
47. Zaplotnik, Rev. Johannes Leo, J.C.D., De Vicariis Foraneis, X-142 pp., 1927.
48. Duskie, Rev. John Aloysius, A.B., J.C.D., The Canonical Status of the Orientals in the United States, VIII-196 pp., 1928.
49. Hyland, Rev. Francis Edward, J.C.D., Excommunication, Its Nature, Historical Development and Effects, VIII-181 pp., 1928.
50. Reinmann, Rev. Gerald Joseph, O.M.C., J.C.D., The Third Order Secular of Saint Francis, 201 pp., 1928.
51. Schenk, Rev. Francis J., J.C.D., The Matrimonal Impediments of Mixed Religion and Disparity of Cult, XVI-318 pp., 1929.
52. Coady, Rev. John Joseph, S.T.D., J.U.D., A.M., The Appointment of Pastors, VIII-150 pp., 1929.
53. Kay, Rev. Thomas Henry, J.C.D., Competence in Matrimonial Procedure, VIII-164 pp., 1929.
54. Turner, Rev. Sidney Joseph, C.P., J.U.D., The Vow of Poverty, XLIX-217 pp., 1929.
55. Kearney, Rev. Raymond A., A.B., S.T.D., J.C.D., The Principles of Delegation, VII-149 pp., 1929.
56. Conran, Rev. Edward James, A.B., J.C.D., The Interdict, V-163 pp., 1930.
57. O'Neil, Rev. William H., J.C.D., Papal Rescripts of Favor, VII-218 pp., 1930.
58. Bastnagel, Rev. Clement Vincent, J.U.D., The Appointment of Parochial Adjutants and Assistants, XV-257 pp., 1930.
59. Ferry, Rev. William A., A.B., J.C.D., Stole Fees, V-136 pp., 1930.
60. Costello, Rev. John Michael, A.B., J.C.D., Domicile and Quasi-Domicile, VII-201 pp., 1930.

61. Kremer, Rev. Michael Nicholas, A.B., S.T.B., J.C.D., Church Support in the United States, VI-136 pp., 1930.
62. Angula, Rev. Luis, C.M., J.C.D., Legislation de la Iglesia sobre la intencion en la application de la Santa Misa, VII-104 pp., 1931.
63. Frey, Rev. Wolfgang Norbert, O.S.B., A.B., J.C.D., The Act of Religious Profession, VIII-174 pp., 1931.
64. Roberts, Rev. James Brendan, A.B., J.C.D., The Banns of Marriage, XIV-140 pp., 1931.
65. Ryder, Rev. Raymond Aloysius, A.B., J.C.D., Simony, IX-151 pp., 1931.
66. Campagna, Rev. Angelo, Ph.D., J.U.D., Il Vicario Generale del Vescovo, VII-205 pp., 1931.
67. Cox, Rev. Joseph Godfrey, A.B., J.C.D., The Administration of Seminaries, VI-124 pp., 1931.
68. Gregory, Rev. Donald J., J.U.D., The Pauline Privilege, XV-165 pp., 1931.
69. Donohue, Rev. John F., J.C.D., The Impediment of Crime, VII-110 pp., 1931.
70. Dooley, Rev. Eugene A., O.M.I., J.C.D., Church Law on Sacred Relics, IX-143 pp., 1931.
71. Orth, Rev. Clement Raymond, O.M.C., J.C.D., The Approbation of Religious Institutes, 171 pp., 1931.
72. Pernicone, Rev. Joseph M., A.B., J.C.D., The Ecclesiastical Prohibition of Books, XII-267 pp., 1932.
73. Clinton, Rev. Connell, A.B., J.C.D., The Paschal Precept, IX-108 pp., 1932.
74. Donnelly, Rev. Francis B., A.M., S.T.L., J.C.D., The Diocesan Synod, VIII-125 pp., 1932.
75. Torrente, Rev. Camilo, C.M.F., J.C.D., Las Procesiones Sagradas, V-145 pp., 1932.
76. Murphy, Rev. Edwin J., C.PP.S., J.C.D., Suspension Ex Informata Conscientia, XI-122 pp., 1932.
77. MacKenzie, Rev. Eric F., A.M., S.T.L., J.C.D., The Delict of Heresy in its Commission, Penalization, Absolution, VII-124 pp., 1932.
78. Lyons, Rev. Avitus E., S.T.B., J.C.D., The Collegiate Tribunal of First Instance, XI-147 pp., 1932.
79. Connolly, Rev. Thomas A., J.C.D., Appeals, XI-195 pp., 1932.
80. Sangmeister, Rev. Joseph V., A.B., J.C.D., Force and Fear as Precluding Matrimonial Consent, V-211 pp., 1932.
81. Jaeger, Rev. Leo A., A.B., J.C.D., The Administration of Vacant and Quasi-Vacant Episcopal Sees in the United States, IX-229 pp., 1932.
82. Rimlinger, Rev. Herbert T., J.C.D., Error Invalidating Matrimonial Consent, VII-79 pp., 1932.

83. BARRETT, REV. JOHN D. M., S.S., J.C.D., A Comparative Study of the Councils of Baltimore and the Code of Canon Law, X-223 pp., 1932.
84. CARBERRY, REV. JOHN J., PHD., S.T.D., J.C.D., The Juridical Form of Marriage, X-177 pp., 1934.
85. DOLAN, REV. JOHN L., A.B., J.C.D., The Defensor Vinculi, XII-157 pp., 1934.
86. HANNAN, REV. JEROME D., A.M., S.T.D., LL.B., J.C.D., The Canon Law of Wills, IX-517 pp., 1934.
87. LEMIEUX, REV. DELISE A., A.M., J.C.D., The Sentence in Ecclesiastical Procedure, IX-131 pp., 1934.
88. O'ROURKE, REV. JAMES J., A.B., J.C.D., Parish Registers, VII-109 pp., 1934.
89. TIMLIN, REV. BARTHOLOMEW, O.F.M., A.M., J.C.D., Conditional Matrimonial Consent, X-381 pp., 1934.
90. WAHL, REV. FRANCIS X., A.B., J.C.D., The Matrimonial Impediments of Consanguinity and Affinity, VI-125 pp., 1934.
91. WHITE, REV. ROBERT J., A.B., LL.B., S.T.B., J.C.D., Canonical Ante-Nuptial Promises and the Civil Law, VI-152 pp., 1934.
92. HERRERA, REV. ANTONIO PARRA, O.C.D., J.C.D., Legislacion Ecclesiastica sobra el Ayuno y la Abstinencia, XI-191 pp., 1935.
93. KENNEDY, REV. EDWIN J., J.C.D., The Special Matrimonial Process in Cases of Evident Nullity, X-165 pp., 1935.
94. MANNING, REV. JOHN J., A.B., J.C.D., Presumption of Law in Matrimonial Procedure, XI-111 pp., 1935.
95. MOEDER, REV. JOHN M., J.C.D., The Proper Bishop for Ordination and Dimissorial Letters, VII-135 pp., 1935.
96. O'MARA, REV. WILLIAM A., A.B., J.C.D., Canonical Causes for Matrimonial Dispensations, IX-155 pp., 1935.
97. REILLY, REV. PETER, J.C.D., Residence of Pastors, IX-81 pp., 1935.
98. SMITH, REV. MARINER T,. O.P., S.T.Lr., J.C.D., The Penal Law for Religious, VII-169 pp., 1935.
99. WHALEN REV. DONALD W., A.M., J.C.D., The Value of Testimonial Evidence in Matrimonal Procedure, XIII-297 pp., 1935.
100. CLEARY, REV. JOSEPH F., J.C.D., Canonical Limitations on the Alienation of Church Property, VIII-141 pp., 1936.
101. GLYNN, REV. JOHN C., J.C.D., The Promoter of Justice, XX-337 pp., 1936.
102. BRENNAN, REV. JAMES H., S.S., M.A., S.T.B., J.C.D., The Simple Convalidation of Marriage, VI-135 pp., 1937.
103. BRUNINI, REV. JOSEPH BERNARD, J.C.D., The Clerical Obligations of Canons 139 and 142, X-121 pp., 1937.
104. CONNOR, REV. MAURICE, A.B., J.C.D., The Administrative Removal of Pastors, VIII-159 pp., 1937.
105. GUILFOYLE, REV. MERLIN JOSEPH, J.C.D., Custom, XI-144 pp., 1937.

106. HUGHES, REV. JAMES AUSTIN, A.B., A.M., J.C.D., Witnesses in Criminal Trials of Clerics, IX-140 pp., 1937.
107. JANSEN, REV. RAYMOND J., A.B., S.T.L., J.C.D., Canonical Provisions for Catechetical Instruction, VII-153 pp., 1937.
108. KEALY, REV. JOHN JAMES, A.B., J.C.D., The Introductory Libellus in Church Court Procedure, XI-121 pp., 1937.
109. MCMANUS, REV. JAMES EDWARD, C.SS.R., J.C.D., The Administration of Temporal Goods in Religious Institutes, XVI-196 pp., 1937.
110. MORIARITY, REV. EUGENE JAMES, J.C.D., Oaths in Ecclesiastical Courts, X-115 pp., 1937.
111. RAINIER, REV. ELIGIUS GEORGE, C.SS.R., J.C.D., Suspension of Clerics, XVII-249 pp., 1937.
112. REILLY, REV. THOMAS F., C.SS.R., J.C.D., Visitation of Religious, VI-195 pp., 1938.
113. MORIARITY, REV. FRANCIS E., C.SS.R., J.C.D., The Extraordinary Absolution from Censures, XV-334 pp., 1938.
114. CONNOLLY, REV. NICHOLAS P., J.C.D., The Canonical Erection of Parishes, X-132 pp., 1938.
115. DONOVAN, REV. JAMES JOSEPH, J.C.D., The Pastor's Obligation in Prenuptial Investigation, XII-322 pp., 1938.
116. HARRIGAN, REV. ROBERT J., M.A., S.T.B., J.C.D., The Radical Sanation of Invalid Marriages, VIII-208 pp., 1938.
117. BOFFA, REV. CONRAD HUMBERT, J.C.D., Canonical Provisions for Catholic Schools, VII-211 pp., 1939.
118. PARSONS, REV. ANSCAR JOHN, O.M.Cap., J.C.D., Canonical Elections, XII-236 pp., 1939.
119. REILLY, REV. EDWARD MICHAEL, A.B., J.C.D., The General Norms of Dispensation, XII-156 pp., 1939.
120. RYAN, REV. GERALD ALOYSIUS, A.B., J.C.D., Principles of Episcopal Jurisdiction, XII-172 pp., 1939.
121. BURTON, REV. FRANCIS JAMES, C.S.C., A.B., J.C.D., A Commentary on Canon 1125, X-222 pp., 1940.
122. MIASKIEWICZ, REV. FRANCIS SIGISMUND, J.C.D., Supplied Jurisdiction According to Canon 209, XII-340 pp., 1940.
123. RICE, REV. PATRICK WILLIAM, A.B., J.C.D., Proof of Death in Prenuptial Investigation, VIII-156 pp., 1940.
124. ANGLIN, REV. THOMAS FRANCIS, M.S., J.C.D., The Eucharistic Fast, VIII-183 pp., 1941.
125. COLEMAN, REV. JOHN JEROME, J.C.D., The Minister of Confirmation, VI-153 pp., 1941.
126. DOWNS, REV. JOHN EMMANUEL, A.B., J.C.D., The Concept of Clerical Immunity, XI-163 pp., 1941.
127. ESSWEIN, REV. ANTHONY ALBERT, J.C.D., Extrajudicial Penal Powers of Ecclesiastical Superiors, X-144 pp., 1941.

128. FARREL, REV. BENJAMIN FRANCIS, M.A., S.T.L., J.C.D., The Rights and Duties of the Local Ordinary Regarding Congregations of Women Religious of Pontifical Approval, V-195 pp., 1941.
129. FEENEY, REV. THOMAS JOHN, A.B., S.T.D., J.C.D., Restitutio in Integrum, VI-169 pp., 1941.
130. FINDLEY, REV. STEPHEN WILLIAM, O.S.B., A.B., J.C.D., Canonical Norms Governing the Deposition and Degradation of Clerics, XVII-279 pp., 1941.
131. GOODWINE, REV. JOHN, A.B., S.T.L., J.C.D., The Right of the Church to Acquire Property, VIII-119 pp., 1941.
132. HESTON, REV. EDWARD LOUIS, C.S.C., PHD., S.T.D., J.C.D., The Alienation of Church Property in the United States, XII-222 pp., 1941.
133. HOGAN, REV. JAMES JOHN, A.B., S.T.L., J.C.D., Judicial Advocates and Procurators, XIII-200 pp., 1941.
134. KEALY, REV. THOMAS M., A.B., Litt.B., J.C.D., Dowry of Women Religious, IX-152 pp., 1941.
135. KEENE, REV. MICHAEL JAMES, O.S.B., J.C.D., Religious Ordinaries and Canon 198, V-164 pp., 1942.
136. KERIN, REV. CHARLES A., S.S., M.A., S.T.B., J.C.D., The Privation of Christian Burial, XVI-279 pp., 1941.
137. LOUIS, REV. WILLIAM FRANCIS, M.A., J.C.D., Diocesan Archives, X-101 pp., 1941.
138. MCDEVITT, REV. GILBERT JOSEPH, A.B., J.C.D., Legitimacy and Legitimation, X-247 pp., 1941.
139. MCDONOUGH, REV. THOMAS JOSEPH, A.B., J.C.D., Apostolic Administrators, X-217 pp., 1941.
140. MEIER, REV. CARL ANTHONY, A.B., J.C.D., Penal Administrative Procedure Against Negligent Pastors, XI-240 pp., 1941.
141. SCHMIDT, REV. JOHN ROGG, A.B., J.C.D., The Principles of Authentic Interpretation in Canon 17 of the Code of Canon Law, XII-331 pp., 1941.
142. SLAFKOSKY, REV. ANDREW LEONARD, A.B., J.C.D., The Canonical Episcopal Visitation of the Diocese, X-197 pp., 1941.
143. SWOBODA, REV. INNOCENT ROBERT, O.F.M., J.C.D., Ignorance in Relation to the Imputability of Delicts, IX-271 pp., 1941.
144. DUBÉ, REV. ARTHUR JOSEPH, A.B., J.C.D., The General Principles for the Reckoning of Time in Canon Law, VIII-299 pp., 1941.
145. MCBRIDE, REV. JAMES T., A.B., J.C.D., Incardination and Excardination of Seculars, XX-585 pp., 1941.
146. KRÓL, REV. JOHN T., J.C.D., The Defendant in Ecclesiastical Trials, XII-207 pp., 1942.
147. COMYNS, REV. JOSEPH J., C.SS.R., A.B., J.C.D., Papal and Episcopal Administration of Church Property, XIV-155 pp., 1942.

148. Barry, Rev. Garrett Francis, O.M.I., J.C.D., Violation of the Cloister, XII-260 pp., 1942.

149. Bolduc, Rev. Gatien, C.S.V., A.B., S.T.L., J.C.D., Les Études dans les Religions Clèricales, VIII-155 pp., 1942.

150. Boyle, Rev. David John, M.A., J.C.D., The Juridic Effects of Moral Certitude on Pre-Nuptial Guarantees, XII-188 pp., 1942.

151. Canavan, Rev. Walter Joseph, M.A., Litt.D., J.C.D., The Profession of Faith, XII-143 pp., 1942.

152. Desrochers, Rev. Bruno, A.B., Ph.L., S.T.B., J.C.D., Le Premier Concile Plènier de Quebéc et le Code de Droit Canonique, XIV-186 pp., 1942.

153. Dillon, Rev. Robert Edward, A.B., J.C.D., Common Law Marriage, X-148 pp., 1942.

154. Dodwell, Rev. Edward John, Ph.D., S.T.B., J.C.D., The Time and Place for the Celebration of Marriage, X-156 pp., 1942.

155. Donnellan, Rev. Thomas Andrew, A.B., J.C.D., The Obligation of the Missa pro Populo, VII-131 pp., 1942.

156. Eltz, Rev. Louis Anthony, A.B., J.C.D., Cooperation in Crime, XII-208 pp., 1942.

157. Gass, Rev. Sylvester Francis, M.A., J.C.D., Ecclesiastical Pensions, XI-206 pp., 1942.

158. Guiniven, Rev. John Joseph, C.SS.R., J.C.D., The Precept of Hearing Mass, XIV-188 pp., 1942.

159. Gulczynski, Rev. John Theophilus, J.C.D., The Desecration and Violation of Churches, X-126 pp., 1942.

160. Hammil, Rev. John Leo, M.A., J.C.D., The Obligations of the Traveler According to Canon 14, VIII-204 pp., 1942.

161. Haydt, Rev. John Joseph, A.B., J.C.D., Reserved Benefices, XI-148 pp., 1942.

162. Huser, Rev. Roger John, O.F.M., A.B., J.C.D., The Crime of Abortion in Canon Law, XII-187 pp., 1942.

163. Kearney, Rev. Francis Patrick, A.B., S.T.L., J.C.D., The Principles of Canon 1127, X-162 pp., 1942.

164. Linahen, Rev. Leo James, S.T.L., J.C.D., De Absolutione Complicis In Peccato Turpi, 114 pp., 1942.

165. McCloskey, Rev. Joseph Aloysius, A.B., J.C.D., The Subject of Ecclesiastical Law According to Canon 12, XVII-246 pp., 1942.

166. O'Neil, Rev. Francis Joseph, C.SS.R., J.C.D., The Dismissal of Religious in Temporary Vows, XIII-220 pp., 1942.

167. Prince, Rev. John Edward, A.B., S.T.B., J.C.D., The Diocesan Chancellor, X-136 pp., 1942.

168. Riesner, Rev. Albert Joseph, C.SS.R., J.C.D., Apostates and Fugitives from Religious Institutes, IX-168 pp., 1942.

169. Stenger, Rev. Joseph Bernard, J.C.D., The Mortgaging of Church Property, 186 pp., 1942.
170. Waldron, Rev. Joseph Francis, A.B., J.C.D., The Minister of Baptism, XII-197 pp., 1942.
171. Willett, Rev. Robert Albert, J.C.D., The Probative Value of Documents in Ecclesiastical Trials, X-124 pp., 1942.
172. Woeber, Rev. Edward Martin, M.A., J.C.D., The Interpollations, XII-161 pp., 1942.
173. Benko, Rev. Matthew Aloysius, O.S.B., M.A., J.C.D., The Abbot *Nullius*, XV-147 pp., 1943.
174. Christ, Rev. Joseph James, M.A., S.T.L., J.C.D., Dispensation from Vindicative Penalties, XIII-285 pp., 1943.
175. Clancy, Rev. Patrick M. J., O.P., A.B., S.T.Lr., J.C.D., The Local Religious Superior, X-229 pp., 1943.
176. Clarke, Rev. Thomas James, J.C.D., Parish Societies, XII-147 pp., 1943.
177. Connolly, Rev. John Patrick, S.T.L., J.C.D., Synodal Examiners and Parish Priest Consultors, X-223 pp., 1943.
178. Drumm, Rev. William Martin, A.B., J.C.D., Hospital Chaplains, XII-175 pp., 1943.
179. Flanagan, Rev. Bernard Joseph, A.B., S.T.L., J.C.D., The Canonical Erection of Religious Houses, X-147 pp., 1943.
180. Kelleher, Rev. Stephen Joseph, A.B., S.T.B., J.C.D., Discussions with non-Catholics: Canonical Legislation, X-93 pp., 1943.
181. Lewis, Rev. Gordian, C.P., J.C.D., Chapters in Religious Institutes, XII-169 pp., 1943.
182. Marx, Rev. Adolph, J.C.D., The Declaration of Nullity of Marriages Contracted Outside the Church, X-151 pp., 1943.
183. Matulenas, Rev. Raymond Anthony, O.S.B., A.B., J.C.D., Communication, a Source of Privileges, XII-225 pp., 1943.
184. O'Leary, Rev. Charles Gerard, C.SS.R., J.C.D., Religious Dismissed After Perpetual Profession, X-213 pp., 1943.
185. Power, Rev. Cornelius Michael, J.C.D., The Blessing of Cemeteries, XII-231 pp., 1943.
186. Shuhler, Rev. Ralph Vincent, O.S.A., J.C.D., Privileges of Religious to Absolve and Dispense, XII-195 pp., 1943.
187. Ziolkowski, Rev. Thaddeus Stanislaus, A.B., J.C.D., The Consecration and Blessing of Churches, XII-151 pp., 1943.
188. Heneghan, Rev. John Joseph, S.T.D., J.C.D., The Marriages of Unworthy Catholics: Canons 1065 and 1066, XVI-213 pp., 1944.
189. Carroll, Rev. Coleman Francis, M.A., S.T.L., J.C.L., Charitable Institutions.
190. Ciesluk, Rev. Joseph Edward, Ph.B., S.T.L., J.C.L., National Parishes in the United States, VI-178 pp., 1944.

191. Coburn, Rev. Vincent Paul, A.B., J.C.D., Marriages of Conscience, XII-172 pp., 1944.

192. Connors, Rev. Charles Paul, C.S.Sp., A.B., J.C.D., Extra-Judicial Procurators in the Code of Canon Law, X-94 pp., 1944.

193. Coyle, Rev. Paul Raymond, A.B., J.C.D., Judicial Exemptions, X-142 pp., 1944.

194. Fair, Rev. Bartholomew Francis, A.B., S.T.L., J.C.D., The Impediment of Abduction, XII-122 pp., 1944.

195. Gallagher, Rev. Thomas Raphael, O.P., A.B., S.T.Lr., J.C.D., The Examination of the Qualities of the Ordinand, X-166 pp., 1944.

196. Gannon, Rev. John Mark, S.T.L., J.C.D., The Interstices Required for the Promotion to Orders, XII-100 pp., 1944.

197. Goldsmith, Rev. J. William, B.C.S., S.T.L., J.C.D., The Competence of Church and State over Marriage—Disputed Points, X-128 pp., 1944.

198. Goodwine, Rev. Joseph Gerard, A.B., S.T.B., J.C.D., The Reception of Converts, XIV-326 pp., 1944.

199. Kowalski, Rev. Romuald Eugene, O.F.M., A.B., J.C.D., Sustenance of Religious Houses of Regulars, X-174 pp., 1944.

200. McCoy, Rev. Alan Edward, O.F.M., J.C.D., Force and Fear in Relation to Delictual Imputability and Penal Responsibility, XII-160 pp., 1944.

201. McDevitt, Rev. Vincent John, Ph.B., S.T.L., J.C.L., Perjury.

202. Martin, Rev. Thomas Owen, Ph.D., S.T.D., J.C.D., Adverse Posession, Prescription and Limitation of Actions: The Canonical "Praescriptio," XX-208 pp., 1944.

203. Miklosovic, Rev. Paul John, A.B., J.C.L., Attempted Marriages and Their Consequent Juridic Effects.

204. Mundy, Rev. Thomas Maurice, A.B., S.T.L., J.C.D., The Union of Parishes, X-164 pp., 1944.

205. O'Dea, Rev. John Coyle, A.B., J.C.D., The Matrimonial Impediment of Nonage, VIII-126 pp., 1944.

206. Olalia, Rev. Alexander Ayson, S.T.L., J.C.D., A Comparative Study of the Christian Constitution of States and the Constitution of the Philippine Commonwealth, XII-136 pp., 1944.

207. Poisson, Rev. Pierre-Marie, C.S.C., A.B., Ph.L., Th.L., J.C.L., Droits Patrimoniaux des Maisons et des Églises Religieuses.

208. Stadalnikas, Rev. Casimir Joseph, M.I.C., J.C.D., Reservation of Censures, X-141 pp., 1944.

209. Sullivan, Rev. Eugene Henry, S.T.L., J.C.D., Proof of the Reception of the Sacraments, X-165 pp., 1944.

210. Vaughan, Rev. William Edward, J.C.D., Constitutions for Diocesan Courts, X-210 pp., 1944.

211. Paro, Rev. Gino, S.T.D., J.C.L., The Right of Apostolic Delegation, X-221 pp., 1947.

212. BALZER, REV. RALPH FRANCIS, C.P., J.C.D., The Computation of Time in a Canonical Novitiate, X-227 pp., 1945.

213. DOUGHERTY, REV. JOHN WHELAN, A.B., S.T.L., J.C.D., De Inquisitione Speciali, XII-195 pp., 1945.

214. DZIOB, REV. MICHAEL WALTER, J.C.D., The Sacred Congregation for the Oriental Church, XII-181 pp., 1945.

215. EIDENSCHINK, REV. JOHN ALBERT, O.S.B., B.A., J.C.D., The Election of Bishops in the Letters of Pope Gregory the Great, VIII-200 pp., 1945.

216. GILL, REV. NICHOLAS, C.P., J.C.D., The Spiritual Prefect in Clerical Religious Houses of Study, X-140 pp., 1945.

217. HYNES, REV. HARRY GERARD, S.T.L., J.C.D., The Privileges of Cardinals, XII-183 pp., 1945.

218. MCDEVITT, REV. GERALD VINCENT, S.T.L., J.C.D., The Renunciation of an Ecclesiastical Office, XIV-179, pp., 1945.

219. MANNING, REV. JOSEPH LEROY, J.C.D., The Free Conferral of Offices, VIII-116 pp., 1945.

220. MEYER, REV. LOUIS G., O.S.B., A.B., S.T.B., J.C.D., Alms-gathering by Religious, XII-163 pp., 1945.

221. O'DONNELL, REV. CLETUS FRANCIS, M.A., J.C.D., The Marriage of Minors, XII-268 pp., 1945.

222. PRUNSKIS, REV. JOSEPH, J.C.D., Comparative Law, Ecclesiastical and Civil, in Lithuanian Concordat, X-161 pp., 1945.

223. SWEENEY, REV. FRANCIS PATRICK, C.SS.R., J.C.D., The Reduction of Clerics to the Lay State, X-199 pp., 1945.

224. VOGELPOHL, REV. HENRY JOHN, J.C.D., The Simple Impediments to Holy Orders, XVI-190 pp., 1945.

225. BROCKHAUS, REV. THOMAS AQUINAS, O.S.B., J.C.D., Religious who are known as *Conversi*, X-127 pp., 1945.

226. GRIESE, REV. N. ORVILLE, The Marriage Contract and the Procreation of Offspring, XVI-224 pp., 1945.

227. BOUDREAUX, REV. WARREN LOUIS, J.C.L., The *"ab acatholicis nati"* of Canon 1099, § 2, XII-110 pp., 1946.

228. BOWE, REV. THOMAS JOSEPH, A.B., J.C.L., Religious Superioresses, VIII-206 pp., 1946.

229. DIEDERICHS, REV. MICHAEL FERDINAND, S.C.J., J.C.D., The Jurisdiction of the Latin Ordinaries over their Oriental Subjects, XIV-153 pp., 1946.

230. DINGMAN, REV. MAURICE JOHN, A.B., S.T.L., J.C.L., The Plaintiff in Contentious Trials.

231. FRISON, REV. BASIL, C.M.F., M.MUS., J.C.D., The Retroactivity of Law, X-221 pp., 1946.

232. GALVIN, REV. WILLIAM ANTHONY, M.A., J.C.D., The Administrative Transfer of Pastors, XII-288 pp., 1946.

233. GORACY, REV. JOSEPH C., J.C.L., The Diriment Matrimonial Impediment of Major Orders.

234. HALE, REV. JOSEPH FRANCIS, M.A., S.T.L., J.C.L., The Pastor of Burial.

235. HENRY, REV. JOSEPH ARTHUR, A.B., J.C.D., The Mass and Holy Communion: Inter-Ritual Law, XII-138 pp., 1946.

236. LINENBERGER, REV. HERBERT, C.PP.S., J.C.L., The False Denunciation of an Innocent Confessor.

237. LOWRY, REV. JAMES MARTIN, A.B., J.C.L., Dispensation from Private Vows, XII-216 pp., 1946.

238. LYNCH, REV. GEORGE EDWARD, A.B., S.T.L., J.C.D., Coadjutors and Auxiliaries of Bishops, X-107 pp., 1947.

239. LYNCH, REV. TIMOTHY, M.S.SS.T., J.C.L., Contracts between Bishops and Religious Congregations, XIII-232 pp., 1946.

240. McCLUNN, REV. JUSTIN DAVID, A.B., S.T.L., J.C.D., Administrative Recourse, VII-142 pp., 1946.

241. LOHMULLER, REV. MARTIN NICHOLAS, A.B., J.C.D., The Promulgation of Law, XI-139 pp., 1947.

242. McGRATH, REV. JAMES, A.B., J.C.D., The Privilege of the Canon, XII-156 pp., 1946.

243. MARBACH, REV. JOSEPH FRANCIS, A.B., J.C.D., Marriage Legislation for the Catholics of the Oriental Rites in the United States and Canada, XIV-314 pp., 1946.

244. SHIMKUS, REV. BERNARD ALOYSIUS, A.B., J.C.L., The Determination and Transfer of Rite.

245. SMITH, REV. VINCENT MICHAEL, A.B., S.T.L., J.C.L., Ignorance Affecting Matrimonial Consent.

246. WACHTRLE, REV. PAUL ANTHONY, A.B., J.C.L., The Baptism of the Children of Non-Catholics.

247. CROTTY, REV. MATTHEW M., J.C.L., The Recipient of First Holy Communion, X-142 pp., 1947.

248. EAGLETON, REV. GEORGE, J.C.L., The Quinquennial Faculties, Formula IV, XIV-199 pp., 1948.

249. GIBBONS, REV. MARION L., C.M., LL.B., J.C.L., Domicile of the Wife Unlawfully Separated from Her Husband, XIV-171 pp., 1947.

250. KELLY, REV. BERNARD M., S.T.L., J.C.L., The Functions Reserved to Pastors, IX-141 pp., 1947.

251. KILCULLEN, REV. THOMAS J., LL.M., J.C.L., The Collegiate Moral Person as Party Litigant, X-150 pp., 1947.

252. LAFONTAINE, REV. GERMAIN J., W.F., J.C.L., Relatiens Canoniques entre le Missionnaire et Ses Superieurs.

253. LANE, REV. LORAS T., A.B., S.T.L., J.C.L., Matrimonial Procedure in the Ordinary Court of Second Instance.

254. LOVER, REV. JAMES F., C.SS.R., J.C.L., The Master of Novices, X-168 pp., 1947.

255. McNicholas, Rev. Timothy J., J.C.L., The *Septimae Manus* Witness.
256. Marositz, Rev. Joseph J., M.S.C., J.C.D., Obligations and Privileges of Religious Promoted to the Episcopal or Cardinalitial Dignities, XII-180 pp., 1947.
257. Murphy, Rev. Francis J., A.B., J.C.D., Legislative Powers of the Provincial Council, XII-158 pp., 1947.
258. O'Brien, Rev. Romaeus W., O.Carm., J.C.D., The Provincial Superior in Religious Orders of Men, X-294 pp., 1947.
259. Pfaller, Rev. Benedict A., O.S.B., J.C.D., The *Ipso facto* Effected Dismissal of Religious, XII-225 pp., 1947.
260. Popek, Rev. Alphonse S., M.A., J.C.D., The Rights and Obligations of Metropolitans, XX-460 pp., 1947.
261. Ristuccia, Rev. Bernard J., C.M., J.C.L., Quasi-Religious.
262. Sonntag, Rev. Nathaniel L., O.F.M.Cap., J.C.D., Censorship of Special Classes of Books, XII-147 pp., 1947.
263. Stadler, Rev. Joseph N., J.C.D., Frequent Holy Communion, X-158 pp., 1947.
264. Szal, Rev. Ignatius J., J.C.D., The Communication of Catholics with Schismatics, XII-217 pp., 1947.
265. Wagner, Rev. Urban S., O.F.M.Conv., J.C.L., Parochial Substitute Vicars and Supplying Priests.
266. Quinn, Rev. Joseph, M.A., J.C.D., Documents Required for the Reception of Orders, XII-207 pp., 1948.
267. Bennington, Rev. James Clement, A.B., J.C.L., The Recipient of Confirmation.
268. Blaher, Rev. Damian Joseph, O.F.M., A.B., J.C.L., The Ordinary Processes in Causes of Beatification and Canonization.
269. Clune, Rev. Robert Bell, B.A., J.C.L., The Judicial Interrogation of the Parties.
270. Courtemanche, Rev. Basil F., B.A., J.C.L., The Total Simulation of Matrimonial Consent.
271. Dlouhy, Rev. Maur John, O.S.B., A.B., J.C.L., The Ordination of Exempt Religious.
272. Donovan, Rev. John Thomas, Ph.B., S.T.L., J.C.L., The Clerical Obligations of Canons 138 and 140.
273. Freking, Rev. Frederick W., A.B., S.T.B., J.C.L., The Canonical Installation of Pastors.
274. Fulton, Rev. Thomas B., J.C.L., Prenuptial Investigation.
275. Godley, Rev. James P., J.C.L., The Time and the Place for the Celebration of Mass.
276. Kane, Rev. Thomas A., A.B., B.S., J.C.L., Jurisdiction of Patriarchs until 1439.
277. Kennedy, Rev. Andrew A., J.C.L., The Annual Pastoral Report to the Local Ordinary.

278. KONRAD, REV. JOSEPH GEORGE, J.C.L., Transfer of Religious.
279. KRESS, REV. ALPHONSE, J.C.L., Contumacy in Ecclesiastical Trials.
280. MCCARTNEY, REV. MARCELLUS ANTHONY, O.F.M., M.A., J.C.L., Faculties of Regular Confessors.
281. MCCASLIN, REV. EDWARD PATRICK, M.A., S.T.L., J.C.L., The Division of Parishes.
282. MCELROY, REV. FRANCIS J., A.B., J.C.L., The Privileges of Bishops.
283. QUINN, REV. STEPHEN, M.S.SS.T., J.C.L., Relation between the Local Ordinary and Religious of Diocesan Approval.
284. SCHNEIDER, REV. EDELHARD LOUIS, A.D.S., M.A., J.C.D., The Status of Secularized Ex-Religious Clerics, X-155 pp., 1948.
285. THOMPSON, REV. CHESTER J., A.B., J.C.L., The Simple Removal from Office.
286. O'BRIEN, REV. KENNETH R., A.B., J.C.D., The Nature of Support of Diocesan Priests in the United States, XVI-162 pp., 1949.
287. METZ, REV. JOHN E., S.T.L., J.C.D., The Recording Judge in the Ecclesiastical Collegiate Tribunal, X-130 pp., 1949.

www.ingramcontent.com/pod-product-compliance
Lightning Source LLC
LaVergne TN
LVHW050205080826
844660LV00012B/354

* 9 7 8 0 8 1 3 2 2 4 2 4 4 *